CW01064523

CLEAN

WINDOWS

MAXINE SUE FELLER
and R.A FELLER

508 West 26th Street KEARNEY, NE 68848
402-819-3224
info@medialiteraryexcellence.com

ABOUT THE AUTHOR

Appreciating each other's works as writers, a mother and son decided to team up and write a book together to try to overcome the misery of their lost relationship to heal old wounds and disagreements.

Healing undertones on this journey of coming together is reflected in the story of "Clean Windows." Most experience economic circumstances where parents of children have to go to work and leave behind teens to find their own way. At this time, the knot of family unity becomes untied.

After the success of Maxine's book, "The Fortunate Child," she took notice of her son being an award-winning writer as well. Despite R. A. Feller's finding his way through street gangs, drugs, and odd jobs, he was able to write the Calington Castle 10-book series where he found healing by learning to love the truth.

"Clean Windows" is a good, enjoyable story that brings hope and freshness to life.

CONTENTS

Chapter 1

Mr. and Mrs. Carlos Lopez awoke early in the morning to the sound of the crowing "Cock-a-doodle doo." The rooster lived on the farm down the road. He was heard each morning at the rented house where they lived in sunny Puerto Rico.

"Good morning, Maria," said Carlos.

His shapely wife gave him a pleasant kiss to brighten his day.

"Ah, life is good."

He looks at his wife and says, "Being with you is such a blessing."

Getting out of bed, he goes into the shower and starts to sing. Maria rises, pulls on her robe, and goes to the kitchen to fix breakfast.

The front door creaks open and their sixteen-year-old son, Georgio, enters with Spark. Their black dog that has a white lightning streak on its chest is how he got his name.

"Good morning, Mom. Have you told dad about Raphie flunking out of school yet?"

"Shhh! No, and don't say anything about it to your father while you two are riding on the road. Raphie's father will insist his son work in his store, and that might be upsetting to your father. After you get back tonight, I have a surprise for you both."

"A surprise? Please tell me what it is."

"Georgio, my straight-A student… What kind of question is that?"

"Well, what is it?"

"You know if I tell you then it wouldn't be a surprise. Put Spark in your room so we can sit and eat in peace."

"Could you give me a hint?"

Maria whispers, "It ties in with what you've been telling me about Raphie having so much trouble with his school work. Go and put Spark away now, you know Papa doesn't like to be kept waiting at the table."

Carlos enters the kitchen whistling and says, "I can't wait to get out on the open road to stretch my legs on my bicycle. Ah, the cool morning air coming off the ocean, and that final coast down the road into town… it's so refreshing to the soul."

Maria places the scrambled eggs and toast on the table, and pieces of orange for each. After she sits down, they join hands. Papa prays, "Lord, thank you for the food we are about to receive." All say, "Amen." Giorgio smiles with the thought, *"Another bicycle race with Papa."*

***

Out on the road to town, their pedals blaze and the wheels spin like they're going to fly off. The two ride into the ocean breeze. This keeps Carlos and his son cool during their race. This morning, it is Georgio who reaches the top of the hill first, beating his father by a full wheel.

After catching his breath, Georgio says in a jovial way, "I guess you're getting old, Papa."

Carlos replies, "No. You're getting stronger, unless you forgot to bring all your books."

"No. They're all in there, Papa."

Having caught their breath, the two give each other an affectionate hug before they part ways. Georgio goes off to the schoolhouse at the top of the hill, while his father goes down the road to town.

***

When Lopez arrives at work, he notices that a new sign has been put up over the storefront. It reads: *Rivera & Son, General store*. He's glad that his boss's son, Raphie, is going to work at the store one day.

However, Carlos is surprised to see Raphie sweeping up the front porch of the store. "Hey Raphie, how come you're not in school?"

"Good morning, Mr. Lopez. You best go inside, my dad wants to talk with you."

Walking into the store, Carlos sees that Mr. Rivera has a stern expression on his face. "I'm sorry to tell you, Carlos, but I'm going to have to let you go at the end of the month."

"Isn't there some way you could keep me on 'till I find another job, Mr. Rivera? I'll help you, and train your son in the meantime."

"That's why you're staying on till the end of the month."

"It hurts to hear you say it like that, Mr. Rivera. I've been here with you for twenty years. Good business relations are worth as much as the goods on the shelf."

"Carlos, I'm aware good jobs are scarce on this island. You know as well as I that the customers will come here for the goods. Besides, it's up to me to train my son thoroughly after you're gone. It will be a good bonding time for the two of us."

"I'm glad for you, Mr. Rivera, but isn't there anything you can do for me? My loyalty should be worth something to you."

"You're right. Carlos. Hmm… I believe I have an idea to get you started in the right direction. Why not try your luck in the States? You've been a very good employee. You should have no trouble getting a job… or perhaps you might start a business of your own. I will write a letter of reference to help you, but that's the best I can do."

"Ay Dios mios! The end of the month is only two weeks away."

Mr. Rivera tries to encourage him further by saying, "If God is for us…"

Carlos remembers, "Then what can stand against us?"

"You're a good man, Carlos. I'm sure God will guide you."

Chapter 2

Arriving at the house in the evening, Maria sees that Carlos looks troubled. He's not his usual cheerful self. So, she asks, "What's wrong, Carlos?"

"I'll be losing my job at the end of this month to make room for the boss's son at his business."

"Don't trouble yourself over that. God is with us."

"That's what Mr. Rivera said to encourage me."

"Well, he's right."

"Woman, there are no jobs available on this island as good as the one I have now to support us."

"Carlos, who is in control?"

"I thought it was me."

"No, that's where you're wrong."

"What do you mean?"

"Do you love me?"

"Of course! And your love for me holds us on course."

Maria responds, "Just as we trust one another and have faith in our Lord."

"Why are we having this conversation?"

"Have faith and trust me."

"You're sitting there smiling like a cat who swallowed a canary. You either heard from God or have done something that I don't know about yet?"

"Let's just say a little bit of both."

"What do you mean?"

"I had my suspicions about what might happen at your place of business if Raphie was dropped from the school. So, I wrote to my Uncle George.

You know… the one who visited us, and lives on the Mainland. We named Georgio after him."

"What did you write to him about?"

"Let's call it a woman's intuition and God's guidance combined. Now, before you say another word, I want you to take a look at what's in this envelope." Taking a white envelope from her apron pocket, she hands it to him.

Upon opening it, he sees three plane tickets along with cash enough for them to leave and go to the United States. Carlos is shocked as he happily looks them over. "These tickets are dated for the end of the month, a week after Georgio's school closes. Now, I too feel like a cat that has swallowed a canary." He goes and hugs her with tears in his eyes.

Carlos is still holding the envelope and tickets in his hand when the door creaks open and Georgio enters with the dog. "Sorry I got back late with Spark. I see that you two are smiling. Papa, what was the surprise Mama showed you?"

"We're going to leave Puerto Rico and move to New York. We'll be staying with your Uncle George in the Bronx at the end of this month since your papa no longer works for Mr. Ravera."

Chapter 3

At the airport, the Lopez family boards a large commercial airliner. Georgio's mother takes hold of her husband's hand to pray as he watches the plane take off through his window.

The realization that he is leaving Puerto Rico, and the life he has known causes Georgio to look at his Mama and Papa with concern. He's leaving all his friends behind. His parents are the only people he now knows.

Leaving his beloved Spark behind was the hardest thing of all. The pet had been his main companion, but they'd informed him that no dogs were allowed where they were going to live. Sadly, he gave Spark to one of his friends.

During the flight, the hum of the engines made him drowsy. He recalled many happy times of being with his friends.

Passing higher into the clouded kingdom of the sky, he feels more alone. He's sad to have left behind his friends and the island he knew. He doesn't know what to expect in the future. He'd understood his culture. *What would be expected of him now in this new place he was heading? He wondered if he would be able to fit in."*

***

Soon Georgio becomes intrigued by this situation and his mood soon changes. He thinks of himself as being a child again. He's eager to learn. He'd never flown in a plane before. Flying over this new country, everything below looks so tiny.

***

Arriving at the outskirts of the city, he saw that the buildings were larger and taller than he'd ever seen before. Then there was an announcement over the intercom that the plane was going to land. They were instructed to gather their belongings after their arrival. Mama squeezed down on his fingers as the plane bounced on its wheels before gliding to a stop. They were now at John F. Kennedy Airport in New York City. When Georgio sees all the people who he doesn't know, he feels like a stranger in a new world. He holds on tightly to the hands of his parents. Carlos feels uncertain too, and understands his son's look of anxiety. He says, "Be brave, son. 'For if God is with us, then what can stand against us?'"

His attention shifts to the rotating luggage carousel. Getting it was another mini wonder to him. He'd never seen a rotating baggage rack before.

Then they see his mother greet a familiar looking man with a big hug. Georgio smiles when he recognizes him to be his Uncle George from the photo Mama kept on the table. His visit to Puerto Rico was remembered by him.

After that, Georgio gets his hair messed up by Uncle George, and a warm glow comes over his body. He watches his father shake hands with him.

"Welcome to the United States," says Uncle George. Georgio finally feels welcomed in the States.

Chapter 4

In the midst of all the noise and the hustle and bustle, it was a pleasant relief to get into his uncle's quiet car. Looking out the back window, Georgio now felt he belonged in this new country amongst his family. Laying his head on his Papa's shoulder, he sighs. Now relaxed, he finds this new place that first seemed so large and strangely comfortable.

They drove past many streets filled with tall buildings and lots and lots of people. They even drove over a bridge! Looking down into the water, he saw the ships below and his heavy eyelids closed.

***

Uncle George pulled his car up to his two-family house that he had converted into six separate apartments; thereby bringing in rental money that covered all his expenses.

George had worked hard to establish himself. He was now ready to share the fruits of his labor with his sister and brother-in-law who were in need.

At first, there had been a bit of arguing with his wife, but after a while, even she agreed that it was the right thing to do. He rang the doorbell to alert his wife, Sandra, that the new members of their family were here. She put on a smile and composed herself, getting ready to meet the family from Puerto Rico. Opening the door, she experienced an outpouring of warmth and love from Maria, as she put her extended arms around her in an embrace.

"Hola mi hermana de, George! I mean, my new sister. It is good to finally meet you."

Sandra felt a little more relaxed, but she remained aloof and standoffish seeing how these people were dressed. Her husband picked up on her tension and said, "My sister really brightens up a room, eh Sandra?"

Sandra nods in agreement, "Yes. She does that indeed."

Carlos steps up and gives her a firm handshake with a big smile, "Hi, I'm Carlos and this is my son Georgio." He takes her hand and shakes it enthusiastically, "Hi!"

George further relaxes the atmosphere by shouting happily, "This is a cause for celebration! Come on, I'll help you get your luggage out of the car. I'll need room for the food and drinks."

"Come on, sis… Oh, by the way, here are the keys to your new apartment. After we get the luggage out, I'll show you which apartment is yours.

Carlos says, "Thanks again for everything."

***

Maria was pleased to see that they would live in the apartment right next door to her brother. They explore their furnished two-bedroom apartment and find there are two bathrooms. Maria chooses the bedroom with the bathroom.

"Well, here's the last suitcase, Maria. Don't worry, I have a feeling that everything's going to work out just fine," says her brother.

***

After unpacking, Carlos throws up his hands, "I cannot believe how the Lord is blessing us. We're in the United States with a furnished apartment and two bathrooms."

Then Maria and Georgio enter the kitchen. Maria starts to cry when she sees all the new appliances. Confused, Georgio runs back to his Papa and says, "Why is Mama crying? Isn't she glad to be here?" Those are happy tears, son. Now, let's all go next door and thank Sandra, our gracious hostess."

Maria agrees, "Yes, we must."

***

At the doorway while ready to leave, George calls to Sandra who's seated with the family in the living room, "Sweetheart, please call Sal's Delicatessen and order some food and a case of beer. I'm going over to pick it up now."

When the strong emotions of gratitude have quieted down, Sandra says with a weak smile and says, "I'm glad that you're pleased with your apartment. I'll fix us all some tea."

***

Suddenly, a rapid series of knocks are heard on the door. Sandra says, "How strange… I'm not expecting anyone, or any deliveries."

She goes to look through the peephole in the door and says to the policeman she sees, "Yes, can I help you?" and then she opens the door.

9

"Does a George Santiogo live here?" He then holds up her husband's wallet... "Do you recognize this?" She nods her head and asks, "Has something happened to my George?"

"There's been a hit and run accident, ma'am. I'm sorry to tell you that we found this wallet next to the driver's dead body in the front seat of the wrecked car.

Witnesses say a truck ran through the stop sign on the corner and hit him, but kept on going. Your husband probably never saw what hit him."

Sandra gasps and puts her hand to her mouth. "Oh no!" She quickly turns and points a wavering finger at the Lopez family, "It's all your fault that this has happened to me! I pleaded with him to send you money and not to invite you into our home... Well, I'm the landlord here now.

Officer, I want you to put those people out of my house!"

Carlos is flabbergasted by this accusation and says "You're upset, Sandra... wait a bit... and we'll talk about this tomorrow."

"If you hadn't come here, this never would have happened!"

Tears fill Maria's eyes while speaking, "We have a key to our apartment next store," Maria says to the officer."

The Police officer says, "If they have a key, ma'am, then legally they're your tenants."

"I own this property now, and I want them out!" The officer says, "You'll have to file an eviction complaint at the courthouse, ma'am," then leaves.

***

In the morning, the Lopez family is awakened by the sound of hammering outside. Looking out the window, they see Sandra is pounding a wooden stake with a "For Sale" sign into the ground on her front lawn. Realizing that Sandra is in pain with her grief, Maria puts on her robe and goes outside to comfort her. She says, "You need your family around you now... Why are you doing this? We're all very upset. I loved my brother, too... and my heart has so much pain. From what we practiced as children, I know he is in a better place. George is with God now."

Refusing to be consoled by her words, Sandra turns and walks back into the house. Maria calls after her, "I shall pray for you!"

She falls to her knees and holding her hands to her eyes, she weeps and prays.

***

Maria is disrupted from her prayers by the sound of a man's voice who yells at her from the sidewalk, "In this neighborhood, we don't argue on the streets. Take your squabbling inside!"

Another man calls out, "Hey lady, how much do you want for your house?"

Maria recalls how friendly and sympathetic people were on the island of Puerto Rico. We were concerned about one another. She continues to ponder, Why, Lord, are these new neighbors such uncaring people?

After recalling a hymn from her early years, she begins to sing, "Lord, help me live from day to day. In such a self-forgetful way. That even when I kneel to pray, my prayer shall be for others today. Let this my motto be, help me to live for others. That I may live like Thee."

Chapter 5

Georgio walks alongside his mother on the warm street. He's checking off another ad in the newspaper under the apartments for rent column. He says, "There's one more address left, and it's not too far from here, Mama."

Maria's head hangs in discouragement as she says, "It's painful for me to live at Sandra's where we are not welcome. Come Georgio, let's go and take a look."

They travel a few more blocks. Stopping at the crosswalk on the busy street corner, they push a button for them to cross. Waiting there,

Georgio reflects on the events of the day, Hmmn. I don't understand why the people we saw didn't take our information, but said we'll consider you if another apartment becomes available. Georgio's thoughts are disrupted by his mother, "Let's hope your father has better luck than us." The light turns green and they find their way to the last address on the newspaper list.

"According to the way you raised me, something tells me it will be God and not luck that will open a door for us to find a place here."

Arriving at the address, Georgio sees a cockroach crawl into a crevice in one of the cracked brick steps at the entry. They climb up many stairs on a rickety wooden staircase painted battleship gray. Reaching the landing where they see the word "Superintendent" printed on the door, they stop and Maria takes a deep breath.

She straightens herself up and knocks. They stand waiting. When the door opens, a tall, heavyset man ogles the beautiful-looking white complexioned woman at his door. He smiles at her and glances over towards the boy. He asks, "How can I help you, ma'am?"

Maria replies with her obvious accent, "We've come about your ad in the newspaper for an apartment."

After a surprised look of momentary shock disappears from his face, he brings up a glob of spit and hits Maria with it in the face. Then he snarls, "We don't want no spics around here!"

Maria holds up her arm, preventing her son from lunging forward to strike him and says, "Georgio! This man is very sick. Remember, our Lord!"

The door is slammed shut in their faces. "Here, Mama, take my handkerchief. Maria wipes her face and says with a trembling voice, "I was afraid he would throw us down the stairs if you tried to fight him."

"You did the right thing stopping me."

"Now that we really understand the situation in this neighborhood, perhaps we'll be better off in an area where other Spanish-speaking people live.

***

Back at the apartment, Maria sees a legal-looking notice taped on the door. She reads it and discovers that it is an eviction notice from the landlord. Taking it down, she enters the apartment and places it on the kitchen table.

She sits down and bows her head to pray. "Oh, Lord of Hosts. Protect Georgio, and be with Carlos in the city today. Please help us in this time of our great need. Please help us to find a place where we can live in peace. Amen."

Georgio arrives carrying two large brown paper bags filled with food from the grocery store. He presses the doorbell with his elbow.

Maria opens the door and says, "Ay Caramba! How much did you spend, Georgio?"

"Don't worry, Mama, the prices here are not as expensive as they were on the island. These groceries were only about fifteen dollars a bag. Here's the change back from your fifty dollars."

Handing the money to her, he says, "It's a good thing Uncle George sent us money along with the airline tickets."

Maria replies, "Perhaps he had a premonition. I recall that when he left on the last day, he said everything would work out fine for us."

"Mama, it's like he was talking about our future here as if he knew."

***

After the groceries are put away, Maria turns to her son and says, "Give your Mama a hug."

She opened her arms and as the two embraced, it soothes them both. Maria looks to her son, "Remember, Georgio, true love will never fail."

The doorbell rings and Georgio says, "That must be Papa."

"Let's hope so." She looks into the peephole and sees her grinning husband. She quickly opens the door and says, "You look like you have good news…"

"Yes! Come and sit down so I can get a better look at your faces when you hear."

"Wow. It must be really good news." She and Georgio sit and eagerly await to hear some good news after their long day of disappointments.

"I got a job in the city today."

Georgio breaks out with a wide smile, "That's great, Papa. Now, all we need to do is find us a place to live."

Maria looks concerned and asks, "What kind of neighborhood is this place where you have your new job?"

"Wait. Before I get into that, let me finish telling you all of my good news"

Maria and Georgio look perplexed as Carlos continues, "My new job comes with a larger apartment than this one. The walls aren't as pretty, but with wallpaper they'll be fine. The appliances aren't as nice, but we'll still have two bathrooms… and the best part about it is… I'll have my own office."

Georgio asks, "What kind of job did you get, Papa?"

"I'll give you a hint, I'm the one people will come to for help."

Maria remains calm after listening to him and asks, "What kind of job is it, Carlos?"

"Maria, God moves in mysterious ways. Do you remember how handy I became back on the island when I had to learn how to fix all the things that went wrong in our rental place? It's a good thing the landlord never did any of those repairs that were needed?"

"You're a superintendent" exclaims Maria. She lumps out of her chair and gives Carlos a big hug."

Georgio asks, "When do you start, Papa?

"At the end of the week."

"That's wonderful, Carlos," says Maria.

"If you feel ambitious, Maria, I'm sure you can get house cleaning work, too."

Maria nods her head and smiles, "There's lots of opportunities here for us. God hasn't forgotten us. Hallelujah!"

"How about me, Papa? Can I go to work, too?"

"Not yet. You must finish your education, my son. You are a very smart boy. I believe that you will become someone of real importance one day. When that time comes, I'm sure there'll be a good job for you, too."

In the midst of her joy, Maria becomes cautious and asks, "What kind of neighborhood is it in, Carlos?"

There's a big park nearby with a castle in it. It's just north of the George Washington bridge."

Georgio gets excited, "Wow! Can we go there now, Papa?"

Carlos replies, "I was hoping you'd say that."

"How did you find that place?" asks Maria.

"After I prayed this morning, I got an idea… I decided the area for me to look in should have the name of George in it. That name seems to be showing us favor, so I started out by taking a bus to go to the George Washington bridge."

Maria and Georgio look at Carlos full of smiles. "On the way, I got hungry, so when I saw a place to eat, I got off the bus. It was a very busy street. There were trains that travel on tracks above the cars on the street they call Broadway, and many buses to take you to other places you'd want to go."

"Then what happened, Papa?"

"After I ate my lunch, I walked to a nearby church to pray for His guidance. It was a very large one. Then, I prayed till I felt at peace. I then got up from my knees and went for a walk to stretch."

Maria gets up to get a drink of water. "Would you like some water, too, Carlos?"

"Yes, please. Then when I left the church, the sun was shining in my eyes. I saw another street that was on an angle which enabled me to get out of the sun. That's when I saw the castle up on the hill in the park. I wanted to get a better look at it, but I didn't realize how far it was. After a while, I looked for a place to sit…"

Maria interrupts him, "So, tell us how you found the job."

"Like I said, the castle was further than I thought, so I sat down on the stoop of a building to rest. While I was sitting there, I noticed the steps were cracked and that weeds were growing out from where the sidewalk met the building."

After taking a glass of water from Maria's hand, he takes a sip.

"Then, I got the idea to go in and see if I could get hired to do some clean-up and repairs for the owner. I climbed the steps to the entry looking for a bell to ring or someone to ask for work on one of the mailboxes when suddenly three men came through the front door. A policeman had hold of one of them…he was really drunk. The other man was yelling, "Get that fired drunken bum off my property.""

Carlos takes another sip and puts the glass down on the table before continuing, "He was taken right past me when I approached the man who seemed to be in charge to find out if he wanted someone to clean up the front of his building and repair the steps. He cocked his head, looked me over, and asked if I was handy with other things, too."

Georgio jumps up, "And you said yes, Papa?"

"Well, I nodded and he said, 'I like a man who knows how to seize an opportunity and thinks fast on his feet. My name is Mr. Cooperman. How would you like to work for me?'"

"What a wonderful story, Carlos," said Maria.

"Did you walk to the castle afterward, Papa?"

"I thought it would be nicer if we all went and saw it together."

Maria went to her husband and hugged him, "I'm so proud of you."

Georgio joins and hugs them both and while in the huddle, he says, "Me too, Papa."

With their suitcases packed, the Lopez family leaves their apartment to go downstairs to the waiting taxi. After hearing the taxi honk, Sandra looks out of her window and smiles. Peeking through the draped window, she sees the Lopez family leaving with their baggage. "Ding dong!" Hearing her doorbell ring, Sandra goes to the door. On seeing Maria through the peephole, she opens it and slithers her extended arm toward her.

Maria then places the key in her hand and leaves without saying a word.

After the taxi cab pulls away, Sandra walks out to the lawn and yanks the "For Sale" sign out of the ground. Then, she smiles and smugly strides back to her home, thinking, "Now, no one can fault me for bringing spics into the neighborhood."

In the cab, Georgio asks, "Why did Sandra get so mean to us, Mama?"

She replies with a sigh, "The woman is upset about the death of her husband and seeks to blame someone for it. She doesn't fully understand how God loves everyone. Beyond this, I don't have all the answers, Georgio. He moves in mysterious ways."

Chapter 6

They easily move into their new furnished apartment. Once everything has been put in its proper place, they leave and start exploring the neighborhood to find a place to buy groceries.

Seeing a church, Georgio suggests they go in. Following him in, they give thanks to the Lord for providing for them. The priest sees the newcomers and walks over to greet them after they finish their prayers.

"Good afternoon, Father," says Carlos.

"We've just moved in not far from here."

"Ah, welcome to the neighborhood. I detect your accent is from Puerto Rico?" Carlos nods in agreement.

"I recently visited that lovely island and remember that the work situation there was not good."

"Yes, it is a very nice place to visit, but a hard place to live nowadays," says Carlos, agreeing with him.

"Father, it's good to meet a friendly face who understands my situation."

"I recall when I came from Ireland. I learned what it is to be a stranger in a strange land, too."

"I've gotten a job as superintendent for Mr. Cooperman. He owns the tall building on the right on Dogan Street. If you ever need a hand, Father, I'll be glad to help you."

"I appreciate your offer, my son, but there are forty apartments in that building. You'll have your hands full. Mass is at eight and eleven on Sunday mornings, I hope to see you there."

Carlos extends his hand to the Father, and they shake.

Maria says, "Thank you for welcoming us, Father. We need to buy groceries now. Can you please tell us how to get to a grocery store from here?"

Leading them to the door, he points out a small store that's in the middle of the block across the street, "That's where I do my shopping."

***

Carlos walks into the living room and sees his son watching the news on T.V. while seated on the sofa. "Georgio, do you recall the hardware store we saw when we got our groceries the other day?"

"Yes, Papa."

"I'd like it if you'd go over there and pick up three gallons of flat white Benjamin Moore paint. I need it to do a job today, but first I must finish some paperwork on my desk and I don't have time to go there…"

"Sure Papa, I'll be glad to help you out."

"Georgio, here is the $20 I received for the paint. I was told it would be no more than $6 a can. Be sure you get a receipt. A tenant requested it and gave me extra money for it. Be sure to count the change."

"Benjamin Moore paint, count change and get a receipt."

"Good boy… When you get back, I'll have a job for you to do today."

"Okay, Papa." Georgia takes the money and puts it in his pocket as he walks out the door.

He notices that people are staring at him and realizes he's the only one around here with a suntan in the neighborhood. It's an awkward feeling. Georgio recalls the sunny island and he longs for his missed friends. He arrives at the hardware store.

Once inside, he notices a display of the $6 paint he's looking for is now on sale for $4.50 a can. The thought occurs to him, Hey, this might be easy money for me if I keep back the information about the sale… I could pocket the difference… if I alter the receipt or say that it got lost.

He hands over the $20 to pay for the paint and collects the receipt. He counts the change and puts it in his pocket. He's still undecided as to what he will do about the money as he leaves the store. Three sly boys see Georgio coming out of the store walking with the paint and size him up to be robbed. They walk behind him, planning a shove and bump to pick his pockets.

Meanwhile, Georgio has decided to do the right thing and give the exact change to his Papa.

Suddenly, the boys see that a police officer has turned the corner of the street. The boys swiftly change their minds about robbing their mark.

***

On returning home, Georgio opens the office door and puts the paint on the floor next to the desk. He puts the receipt and change on top of it. As he's leaving, he notices the large photo calendar Papa hung up.

He recognizes the photo having similarities to their favorite bicycle road, the one they used to race on in Puerto Rico. Immediately, tears come to his eyes and he's homesick. He sits on the chair and stares at the calendar, recalling happy times that he had on the island.

Maria opens the door and sees him. She asks, "Why are you sitting alone in the dark? At least turn on the lights, Georgio."

"I'm feeling sad because I miss my friends."

"Don't worry, you'll soon make new friends when school starts. Remember, you always have a family and we're here for one another."

When Maria turns on the light and sees the money on the desk, she asks. "Where did that money come from?"

"It's the change for Papa from the $20 he gave me to buy the paint."

Carlos arrives with two paint rollers the priest loaned him to be able to work faster than just using a brush.

"Son, I have a job for you if you want it. You can assist me by using one of these rollers. Time is money. We'll paint the apartment now, and if we get it done before the tenant returns, he promised me a bonus. I'll give that to you for your school supplies. Okay?"

"Mama, I'm starting to see that those early lessons of yours are really helping me…"

"What do you mean?"

"God does reward those who are diligent and follow His path."

"Here's another one, 'Show yourself as a friend by being a friend to someone in need. If they love you back, then you've made a friend. We love because God first loved us."

Georgio gives his mother a hug and says, "I love you, Mama."

He leaves with Carlos to earn his needed money.

Monday morning, Maria goes with Georgio to the school to register him. They have no school records with them, so it's decided to give him a battery of tests to determine which grade to place him.

Walking back home, Maria asks, "How do you think you did on those tests?"

"It wasn't very hard for me."

"We'll find out in a few days, the results will come in the mail. I'm glad you feel you did a good job."

Back at the house, Georgio sees Papa at his desk catching up on paperwork, but decides to go in to see him. "Is there something I can do to help you, Papa?"

"Yes. Watch the news and learn about the world we're living in and the nearby areas. It's important for us to know what's going on and look for opportunities for your future."

***

Georgio's grades arrive in the mail. Maria hands him the envelope and says, "This is the beginning of your new life. You should be the first to know where you stand."

He tears open the envelope and reads it. "Mama! I'm a junior in high school."

They hear footsteps in the hall as Carlos approaches. He says, "Papa, I'm now a junior in high school."

Standing in the alcove, his dad says, "You always got straight A's on your report cards. I'm really not surprised. Let's celebrate your achievement by walking to the castle in the park."

***

After climbing the last hill, they see a sign saying "Welcome to the Cloisters," and reading further, they learn that the castle was brought to this location brick by brick from where it once stood in France. Georgio laughs, "Hey, that makes this castle an immigrant like us." They all laugh together.

Chapter 7

On his way to school, Georgio sees a hungry-looking panhandler seated against a building who asks him for a handout. Georgio has no money, but offers him half his sandwich that he has for lunch.

This friendly gesture reminds the man of his son now deceased. He smiles and thanks him. Georgio smiles in return and thinks to himself, I guess I made my first friend today.

Entering the school, he finds his way to his home classroom. There's a sea of other students in the room, and he takes an empty seat. Georgio waits quietly for the teacher to arrive…in this moment of quiet meditation he endures the clammer of the others. "How long will it take for me not to feel like a stranger in a strange land, I wonder?"

He observes the clicky behavior of some of his classmates and surmises it will take him a much longer time than he first thought. He prays for patience.

Suddenly, the bell rings as his teacher enters and goes to write his name on the blackboard. Afterward, he takes a seat and the room becomes quiet.

The teacher leafs through some papers on his desk and looking up, he asks, "Who is Georgio Lopez?" Georgio raises his hand.

"Well, according to your test scores, Georgio, you'll be lifting the class average in this grade. Welcome to the school."

There's a murmur in the room before the teacher lifts his ruler and bangs it on his desk for silence. He then takes attendance by calling on a student he knows and tells her to hand out the Delaney cards to the pupils. Everyone is directed to fill out the card and then another student is asked to collect them and give them to the teacher. Afterwards, the teacher explains departmental procedures in their school to his students.

***

At the end of the day, the bell rings and Georgio is directed by the loud speaker to return to his homeroom. He's looking over his history book and notices several boys who seem to be walking in the same direction as his homeroom. He assumes they're all in the same class.

One of them bumps into Georgio causing his books to fall on the hallway floor. He tries to pick up the books, but the other boys hold them down with their feet. "Please let me have my books," he pleads.

When he bends down to pick them up, one of the boys takes a book and runs off with it. "I need all my books," Georgio calls out and then the boy turns to jeer, "Let's see how good you do without your book, smarty pants!"

***

In the schoolyard several boys try to encircle Georgio when he leaves the school building. He can see the odds are clearly unfavorable to him and decides to run away.

They chase him, but he escapes by climbing over the tall wire fence around the school. He drops to the ground turning his ankle, but is able to limp away and hobbles homeward.

The panhandler he befriended sees him limping and asks, "How come you're limping now, kid?" Upset, Georgio pours out his difficult day to his new friend. After listening, the panhandler says … "If you were in a gang, those boys wouldn't dare to pick on you, or even try to fight with you."

"You mean I would be treated with respect if I was in a gang? How do I get into a gang?"

***

The following day, Georgio notices several boys of varying ages, but all wearing a special T-shirt with the logo "Justice." He wonders if they belong to the same special group.

Is it a gang name or a bible group? "Hmm." He's curious, but decides to wait a bit longer.

***

After weeks of being taunted and beaten, Georgio decides going to school no longer interests him. His ambition has greatly diminished. He feels it's useless for him to go to school any longer. "These people don't like it when I do well."

The idea of quitting school appeals to him. His mother works out of the neighborhood and his papa is over his head with repairs that have piled up because the last superintendent was a lazy drunk. However, he knows his parents would be very disappointed in him if he quit, so he decides to join a gang for his protection and not quit school. He feels his dad probably wouldn't approve of it, but he's unable to think of a better solution. He's fed up with the beatings and taunts from the bullies in the school and the neighborhood.

Georgio decides to follow the advice he'd heard on the street and join a gang. It seems that it's the best way for him to stay in school.

***

At lunchtime, he approaches a younger student wearing a "Justice" t-shirt and tells him that he's interested in joining a good gang.

Edwardo says, "My gang is the best." Georgio is glad to hear him say that. He asks Edwardo if he can join, too. The boy tells Georgio to meet him under the lamp post after dinner on a street corner well known to Georgio.

***

That evening, Georgio walks to the street corner. There he's greeted by Edwardo. Then, the boy tells a young man leaning against the lamp post why this guy has decided to come here tonight.

He walks over to Georgio and asks him if he thinks he's tough enough to be a gang member? Georgio nods and then the guy punches Georgio hard in the stomach. He bends over in pain and another boy hits him… and another… By the time the moon appears, Georgio is on his knees praying for the courage to withstand this initiation. The beatings finally stop.

Georgio looks up to the boy standing above him who says, "My name is Josh. This is our way to see if you're tough enough to become one of us. We don't want no pansies here. We depend on one another with our lives when we fight. Understand?" Georgio nods his head.

"If you're ready to promise to do as you are told, you can join us, but know this… if you ever decide to refuse an order or attempt to leave the gang… then you'll undergo a beating with weapons and not fists. It will be far less friendly than the beating you got from us tonight."

After saying that, Josh tells Edwardo to give Georgio a "Seven and seven," so he mixes the drink in a paper cup out of two bottles from their paper bags.

Returning home, Georgio goes straight to the bathroom, cleans himself up, then falls asleep on his bed. In the morning, he looks in the mirror and sees how terrible he looks from his beating. He thinks to himself, "Oh God, what have I done? Please protect me from further harm."

Georgio knew his parents would be upset to learn that he'd been unable to fit in at school and had to join a gang for his protection from the bullies and the denigrating taunts in the street from the other kids and the neighbors.

At the breakfast table, his mother asks, "Who has hurt you, Georgio?"

His heart sinks as he lies to his parents, "I got mugged last night in the park. After they found out I had no money on me, they beat me up."

"Oh, my Giorgio!" An upset Maria turns and goes to the stove to get the oatmeal to serve him breakfast. Meanwhile, Carlos whispers to him and passes him $5 for protection money in case he gets robbed again.

"Keep this in your pocket and stay with your friends, it's safer," his dad says.

"Thanks, Papa."

"Wait, I'm not finished."

Georgio looks on as his Papa who continues to speak, "Don't walk alone in the park at night."

Finishing his breakfast and coffee, Carlos leaves the table and goes to his office.

After the lecture from his Papa, Georgio gathers his school books while his mother goes to him and hands him $2 to keep in his pocket in case he gets mugged again, before kissing him on the cheek.

"Thanks for the money," he pockets it.

***

Walking to school, Georgio is pleased to know that his parents love him and want him to be safe from harm. However, he feels ill at ease because he has lied to them… But he's glad that he now has $7 in his pocket as there's a special notebook he'd like to own. Also, he'll need money to buy a gang shirt and to replace the school book that was stolen from him. His puffy lip and two black eyes cause a stir amongst his taunters. They easily recognize that Georgio has undergone an initiation into one of the gangs at school. Thus, today is his first peaceful day on the school grounds. The following day, the book that was stolen from him is returned to him with an apology.

Georgio is pleased that being a member of this gang has brought him good results and no one taunts him now or tries to bully him anymore. It's a great relief to him, he's now glad that he joined the gang.

***

In the cafeteria, he's welcomed to sit with his "Justice" brothers and a few girls start to flirt with him. Day by day, he feels even more enthusiastic about being a gang member.

The bruises slowly fade and Georgio enjoys graffiti painting and the camaraderie of his brothers in the gang. It no longer bothers him that cans of paint are stolen to support their habit of a colorful and fun gang activity.

***

No longer harassed, Georgio is able to study and soon his grades quickly improve as he rediscovers the joy of learning.

Chapter 8

On Sunday, Georgio confesses his sins to the priest and does an assigned penance for them. However, on Monday, he's ready to sin again.

Josh takes a liking to Georgio and encourages him to do more muscle building at the gym. Soon, many opportunities present themselves for Georgio to improve his street-fighting strategies in the weeks that follow. A bicycle chain is now his weapon of choice.

Also, having fast hands and deep pockets, stealing spray paint becomes second nature to Georgio. He's able to carry on a conversation and swipe cans while following a shopkeeper down an aisle, which entertains his gang friends who watch from the store front window. A short time later, Josh promotes Georgio to "Protection." He now likes the fact that he's the one who's in control while watching his classmates who had bullied him fearfully hand over their money to him.

It happens slowly at first, but Georgio starts to fail to see people as flesh and blood. A hardness grips him that he originally hated when he was the one being bullied.

***

Josh introduces marijuana to the gang. Smoking the drug numbs them from feeling their feelings. On one occasion while passing a joint around, there was a deadly silence, no laughter… it just felt good to escape their problems and everybody knew not to break this unwritten law.

The gang brothers became like wolves among sheep while keeping each other in line themselves. They all knew that they were vulnerable, although none were brave enough to be honest enough to admit their fears. One had to show toughness… yet they cried deep inside since all were trapped in their lies. Josh says, "Hey guys, if we enjoy smoking marijuana so much, it should be a cinch to turn a profit by selling it on the street."

Edwardo agrees and says, "That's a great idea, but how would we get anybody to try it?"

"Hey, I know," says Georgio.

"How?" asks Corto.

"Yeah, Brain, how?", questions their leader rather gruffly…since Josh was without an idea of his own."

"When my family first came to the States, my Uncle George wanted to celebrate by throwing us a party."

"I like your idea, Georgio."

"Where and when can we have this party?" Edwardo further questions him.

"Anybody else got any ideas?" asks their leader. The boys look at each other… then Josh calls on Georgio.

"How 'bout it, Brian?"

Hesitantly, he answers, "It takes time to get the word out, but using a holiday party would be a good idea."

Corto speaks up, "Halloween is in two weeks."

"We can tell everyone who pays us protection that their money is going to rent a place for the party… and then tell them to bring their friends," says Josh.

Georgio agrees "We'll have a costume party with masks, that way no one will have to worry about being ratted out if they want to try the joints that we'll be passing around."

"And once they try it, they'll want more." Josh pounds his chest with pride, taking credit for Georgio and Corto's ideas.

"Yeah. Who doesn't want to go to a Halloween party?" asks Corto.

Josh turns to Georgio and says, "There's a big yard behind your building through the alley way. See to it that it's ready for the party."

Georgio looks back at his leader, takes a swallow and nods.

***

Papa is fixing cracks in the sidewalk when Georgio sees him. After taking a deep breath, he says, "Papa, would it be okay if me and my friends use the lot behind the building to have a Halloween party?"

"Anything for my straight-A student."

After being able to get permission so easily, a surge of relief came over Georgio. Now all there is for me to do is clean it up and organize a party.

He walks down the alley, which passes through the building to size up what must be done. He then reports back to Josh.

***

"Good," says Josh.

"Now all that needs to be done is to get the word out in school. We'll need to make it sound like it's an appreciation party for supporting our gang. That should help ease any tension from us leaning on them… in case anyone is considering squealing on us."

Georgio says, "While we're on that topic… next time we collect money from the students, it should go towards the Halloween party."

Josh replies, "I need that money to buy marijuana for the party… that stuff ain't cheap. A backyard don't cost us no money."

"If you want to make sure no one will squeal, we should make it a nice party. A tent if it rains, decorations, and a DJ with records and food. Consider it an investment. We might get more recruits for the gang. I'll ask for extra money for the party to assure them a good time… And that money will go for the drug stash."

"You're going places, Georgio… you're going places… but don't you ever forget that you're only a part of my gang" says Josh.

Georgio quickly answers, "I won't."

"Good, I'm glad we understand each other," Josh says.

***

On Halloween Eve, Maria sits in front of the building and awaits for the neighborhood children to come and get the candies she has for them. Also, she notices the parade of costumed teenagers passing by on their way to the party.

Georgio and the gang have all decided to dress as clowns in order to be easily recognizable in case any trouble should start.

Music helps the friendly atmosphere and there's food on the table. The guests are relaxed as they eat or dance. Then, Josh lights up a joint and passes it to Georgio who then hands it to Edwardo. He then hands it to the girl he's dancing with, saying, "Try this… it's great stuff. You're wearing a mask, no one will know. Be cool and take a drag… then pass it around."

Soon, many joints are going around. After that, there's the sound of many giggles. Josh pats Georgio on the back as his plan has been a big success. Money changes hands for more of the marijuana joints and soon the clowns have sold all their stash.

***

At ten thirty, the party breaks up and everyone staggers out of the alleyway now reeking with the strong scent of marijuana.

The unmistakable smell in the air causes Maria to recognize the sweet odor of the drug. Upset, she runs into the house to tell Carlos, and he comforts her.

They go outside and see Georgio appear under the influence while trying to balance a platter of the remaining food.

Carlos says to Maria, "Don't you worry, Georgio is a sensible boy and this is going to stop tonight. Now go inside, pray, and wait for us at the kitchen table."

Maria goes inside while Carlos goes to his son to offer him help. "Georgio, you look tired. Let me take that platter from you while we walk in together."

Josh sees this and figures something is up. Georgio's father says to him, "Georgio needs to come in now, he's had enough excitement for today."

Josh decides to play it cool and says, "Your old man is right. See you tomorrow, Georgio."

The two go into the apartment together as Carlos says, "Open the doors, Georgio."

He opens the front door to the building and then the door to their apartment. He heads toward his room, but his father says, "Please open the fridge door for me and sit down at the table."

Still dressed as a clown, he does what Papa asks. Carlos says to Georgio, "What were you thinking? Or perhaps you weren't… since marijuana makes you stupid. I know this because when me and my friends smoked it, I became stupid! I smartened up when I saw others get into trouble from using it. Georgio, I'm going to give it to you straight. This marijuana smoking stops tonight or you're out of my house. No more pot! If you want to be stupid, you go and be stupid somewhere else!"

A stunned Georgio is shocked before finding words, "You're throwing me out, Papa? But I'm your son!"

"No son of mine is going to smoke pot and live in my house."

"I'm sorry I've disappointed you, Papa. I won't disrespect you, I'll stop now."

"I'm glad that my son is too smart to be a clown... go and get cleaned up."

***

The next day, Josh is surprised when Georgio comes to the meeting place, "Hey, I didn't expect to see you here for at least a week. I thought your old man was going to ground you for sure."

"In a way, he did."

"What do you mean?"

"Remember the other day when you said I was going places and called me, "Brains?"

"Yeah. I did that."

"We're heading in the wrong direction, Josh."

"No, we're not. With all the joints we sold last night, we made back more than double our money. I'm thinking of trying out a new drug that's supposed to get customers hooked... and then they'll have to keep coming back for more! It's called heroin. They gave me some for you and me to try out first."

"My dad told me drugs make you stupid. I had to agree with him. My brain felt like it was foggy when he spoke to me last night, but I got his message."

"We got a good thing going here, Georgio."

"Josh, when I joined the gang, it was for protection from bullies. Marijuana causes me to let down my guard. What's going to happen if we're

31

all high and then we get attacked by another gang? I don't want to quit the gang, but I'm willing to take a beating now when the rest of the gang shows up because we'll all be as good as dead if we continue with the drugs."

"What did you say?"

"I can see myself living on the streets or jail time coming because my old man will kick me out if I continue to smoke. I know Papa loves me and that's more important to me than any drug. Let's be realistic… it's only a matter of time before we get busted… I say let's quit the drugs while we're still ahead."

"What are we gonna do for money?"

"Drugs are a dead-end, Josh. I'll think of something else we can do for money. Don't forget, you're the one who said you thought I was going places, so have faith in your own words and let's see where it leads. There's other ways of making money."

"I like you, Georgio. I'm going to respect what you say this time, but this conversation stays between you and me or you will get beaten. Understood?" They grip hands and give each other a quick hug.

Edwardo sees this quick exchange and asks Corto beside him, "What do you think those two were talking about?"

Josh overhears him and replies, "A better way to run our business."

***

Standing on the sidewalk, Mr. Cooperman looks admiringly at his neat and clean building. Maria comes out of the building carrying a bucket, a sponge, and a cloth. She begins cleaning the light fixtures on either side of the doorway.

Maria notices that the landlord is watching her and stops what she's doing. "Don't stop on my account, Mrs. Lopez. You and Carlos are doing a great job."

"Thank you, Mr. Cooperman."

"Say, I have another building. How'd you like to earn more money cleaning up like you're doing here?"

"Oh, first I will have to check with my husband."

"That's fine… and when you do, tell him that my wife and her friends are looking for a good cleaner to help them, too."

"I'll let you know, Mr. Cooperman," and she returns to cleaning the light fixtures.

Chapter 9

Maria Lopez is tired after cleaning two large luxury apartments in Mr. Cooperman's tall building overlooking the Hudson River. She slowly walks to the bus stop on the street corner. After waiting 10 minutes on the cold windswept corner, she's glad to see a bus arrive.

Quickly, Maria climbs aboard and drops her coins in the entry box. Seeing an empty seat, she heads toward the rear of the bus. However, the woman in the adjoining seat plunks down the child she was holding on her lap onto the empty seat. So, Maria quickly grasps a bus strap hanging above her head to keep from falling when the bus lurches forward as it leaves the stop.

At the next stop, several people get off and she's able to claim a seat for the long ride to her destination. She's very tired and soon dozes off.

***

When Maria awakes, she reaches up and pulls the cord to signal the driver that she wants to get off. It's not Maria's usual stop to get off. However, tonight Maria is going to the delicatessen in the middle of the block to purchase a special kind of salami for her husband. She thinks Carlos would be happier at his birthday party tonight with a Genoa salami treat. Mrs. Cooperman, her seventh-floor employer, was very pleased with the way Maria cleaned her apartment and decorated the table for an important dinner… so she gave her a few extra dollars when she paid her.

That's why she was now able to afford this treat. In the morning, she had no money to purchase something special for her husband's birthday dinner. However, she'd baked a cake and set a festive table before she went to work.

Carlos will be more fond of this Genoa salami than my cake, she thought, and was proud to be able to buy this treat tonight.

***

Maria uses her key to enter the apartment. She sees the sunshine streaming in through her dirt streaked windows. Recalling the complaints of Mrs. Cooperman… and the other ladies because the special window washer can only come to clean every six weeks... Maria had noticed Mrs. Cooperman closed her drapes to hide the dirty windows from her guests.

Suddenly, the idea that she can have clean windows in her apartment while her rich employers didn't, causes Maria to laugh. She quickly changes back into her work clothes.

In good spirits, she begins the work of cleaning her windows. She's certain that the ladies she works for would be envious of her clean windows and this thought causes her to giggle with glee while she works.

***

Georgio arrives home after school. He's planning to do his homework, eat dinner, and then meet the gang. The plan for tonight is to paint graffiti on the trains at the railroad yard.

He's disappointed to see Mama isn't in the kitchen preparing dinner for him. He quickly realizes that he'll be late to meet his friends and wants to hurry her up. "Ma" he yells out, feeling annoyed with her, "Why aren't you making my dinner?"

At that moment, the front door opens and Papa enters carrying a decorated ice cream cake. On seeing it, Georgio recalls it's his dad's birthday.

Carlos asks, "Is your Mama in the kitchen?"

"No."

"Good," says Carlos, and he places the ice cream cake in the freezer.

"Son, I'll go and find her."

Carlos enters the blue bedroom just as Maria finishes cleaning the last window of the apartment. He hurries to help her back inside the room, but she's already on her feet by the time he reaches her.

She says, "Don't kiss me now, sweetheart, I need to take a shower."

"Why did you clean the windows now?"

"The ladies where I work have been complaining about their dirty windows, but now Carlos…see… we have clean windows. Now, I can feel that we are better off than they are," and she laughs.

With a puzzled look, Carlos says, "As long as you're happy."

"Carlos, I bought you Genoa salami. We'll have it with our rice and beans tonight."

"Thank you very much, my rich wife. I'll cook the dinner tonight while you're in the shower."

***

Returning to the kitchen, Carlos sees that his son is making himself a sandwich using all of the Genoa salami. "Stop! You can't have all the salami, Georgio. That's for all of us to share tonight... and not just for you."

"Mama didn't make dinner... I'll be late to meet my friends...I didn't mean to be greedy, Papa."

"Your Mama has cleaned the windows of our apartment to feel that she is richer than the ladies she works for because their windows are still dirty. We'll cook dinner tonight, son."

"Papa, do you know how to cook? I thought only women cooked. It's not a man's job to cook, is it?"

Carlos laughs and says, "The best chefs in the world are men, my son. Do you plan on getting married so you won't starve to death if anything should happen to your Mama?

Son, take hold of this pot and fill it halfway with water while I get the salt and rice out of the cupboard. Tonight, we're cooking dinner for my rich wife." Did Mama inherit some money?"

Carlos laughs and says, "No, she only thinks that she's rich because she has clean windows while the windows of those rich ladies she works for are still dirty... A special window cleaner company needs to be used for the tall buildings. However, he can only come to clean their windows every six weeks."

Georgio responds, "Now I understand."

Chapter 10

Georgio knew he was late, but he saw that his friends were still under the lamppost waiting, so he ran to meet with them on the corner up ahead.

Dominick complains, "Waiting for you, we missed our free ride to the railroad yard. What kept you?" Georgio didn't want to admit to his friends that his dad had taught him how to cook their dinner earlier... So he says, "I'm sorry to be late. Mama got this loco idea into her head that she'd feel richer than the ladies she works for if she cleaned up all the windows in our apartment."

"What d'ya mean?" asks Edwardo.

"The ladies where she works only get their windows cleaned every six weeks. So now... my Mama feels that she's richer than them and it was her crazy idea that made me late."

Josh said, "We're sorry, too. The night watchman at the yard is usually drunk Friday nights. We would've had a clear field to do our spraying while he slept it off."

Suddenly... a man yells out "Hijo mio." And a middle-aged man comes running up to the group of boys.

"What's the matter, Papa?" asked Edwardo.

"Thank God you're here with your nice friends. Mama and I saw the television coverage at the railroad yard tonight. It was terrible... Shooting and fighting! Ambulances came and took away the boys who got shot. Then the police rounded up the rest. Your mama thought one of them was you. I was just on my way to the police station to bail you out... Whew! I'm so glad you're here and safe with your nice friends. I'll tell Mama it wasn't you that she saw. It's good that you stay with sensible boys who obey the law. Here's $10 to buy ice cream for everyone. Don't stay out too late, Edwardo. Goodnight, fellas."

"Caramba! It was lucky for us that your Mama got it into her head to clean the windows tonight," says Corto... the tallest fellow in the group, although they called him Shorty sometimes.

Josh says, "Hombres... cleaning her windows tonight was a great idea. It kept us from getting into trouble. It also tells us where to look for work this summer. If that window cleaner only comes every six weeks... Then, the guy needs more workers. We're all looking for summer jobs."

"I'd much rather make money than go to school," says Edwardo. It was soon agreed that money was more important to them than school.

Georgio suggests, "I'll ask my mother if she knows the name of the window cleaning company."

Josh says, "Don't bother her… look up a window cleaner of tall buildings in the phone book."

Everyone nods their heads, "Yeah," agreeing with their leader. Corto says, "Ain't Josh a great leader!"

Everyone agrees with him that Josh is the right man for the job.

Josh says, "Georgio, I give you the job of calling up the window cleaning company. Make an appointment for us all to apply for jobs.

***

As soon as Georgio returned home, he asked his mother if she knew the name of the window cleaning company the building used where she worked, and she did.

Chapter 11

In the morning, Georgio telephones information to get the phone number of Wally's Clean Windows, and writes it down. He puts on his Sunday shirt and tie. He takes the phone into the bathroom where he rehearses his voice till he finds the right tone in his expression while looking into the cabinet mirror. He then calls the window company.

"Hello" said a gruff voice, "You want to place a work order with my company?"

"No, sir," replies Georgio. "My friends and I want to work for your company."

"Are you afraid of high places?"

"No, sir."

"Are your friends afraid of working at high heights?"

"I don't know."

"I like that you're honest and don't waste my time. You come to 471 West 125 Street in Manhattan, Monday morning at 5:30 A.M. Bring your friends, I'll soon see if you're the right man for the job. Understand? Capisce?"

"Yes, sir. Who do I ask to see?"

"Wally, that's me."

"Thanks for the opportunity to work for you, Mr. Wally."

Georgio hears him chuckle and Wally gently says "Honest, polite, and savvy… Let me see if you'll be on time, too."

***

After dinner the following night, Georgio goes to report to Josh under the lamppost on the corner. Josh grins and as Georgio approaches the assembled group, he asks, "Did you get us jobs?"

"I got us appointments for Monday morning at 5:30 A.M. to be interviewed by the owner, Mr. Wally."

"Good work, Georgio," says Edwardo, and slaps him on the back.

"Is there anything we need to know before we go?"

"Mr. Wally asked me, "Are you afraid of heights?" I told him no. He then asked me if any of my friends were afraid. I told him that I didn't know."

"What's the address?" asks Josh. After he hears the street address, the smile vanishes from his face. He makes himself look worried and begins to pace up and down under the circle of light... Actually, Josh is afraid of high places, but doesn't want to admit it. He believes a leader should show no weakness.

"What's wrong?" asks Georgio and the other boys.

Josh stops pacing and says, "That address is in the heart of our sworn enemy, "The Spades.""

If any one of us sets foot on their turf, he could get his throat slit."

"But we need jobs," says Corto.

"We're not looking for a rumble. At 5:30 in the morning, who is going to be around on the street to spot us?"

"But what if they guard the bus and train stations? What then?" asks Josh.

"Well, what if we took a taxi to the address?" asks Georgio.

Josh stops pacing and slaps Georgio on the back. "That's what we could do, but who has money for the fare?"

"Well, what if we take the train and go to West 125 Street, and then take a cab to that address?" suggests Georgio.

"That just might work," says Josh.

Corto says," I feel dizzy when I look down from the train platform."

Edwardo says, "Cleaning the windows of tall buildings means we'll be working up in the air on a scaffold... Maybe that's why Wally has openings to hire men to work under those conditions."

"Well, who isn't scared to try to work up in the air?" asks Georgio.

"I'll have to think about this," says Juan.

Everyone says, "That's a good idea."

"What if there's an accident?" asks Ricardo.

"I didn't think to ask him about it. You're right, that's a very important question. We'll have to ask Mr. Wally for the answer when we see him" says Georgio.

Chapter 12

Papa hears the alarm go off early Monday morning. He puts on his robe and goes to his son's bedroom and asks, "Where are you going this early in the morning, son?"

"I'm going to a job interview, Papa."

"Are you going to deliver milk?"

Georgio laughs and replies, "No, Papa. I'm going to get a job cleaning windows, school's almost over and I want a summer job."

"Good luck, son. Make sure they have insurance wherever you find work."

***

Only four of the guys in the gang show up to go to the job interview at Wally's company.

Josh is there… but claims that he doesn't want to endanger the other members because he might be recognized by the Spades. He's very pleased with the lie and is glad he doesn't have to admit to any of them that he's afraid of heights.

He tells them, "I don't want to get my throat cut and endanger your lives, fellas. You go to the job interview with Georgio."

Josh pulls out his wallet and makes a loan to Georgio of enough cash for taxi fare to their destination on the West side and wishes them all, "Good luck."

The trio walk to the underground train station.

***

Wally is at work measuring out his special formula of dry ingredients for cleaning windows. He seals the dry mix in a plastic bag and puts it in a large box. When the box is filled, it will be placed at the rear of the store for use by his men, along with a clean bucket.

It was a tedious chore, but it had to be done. Wally felt it was a big waste of his valuable time. However, he didn't trust anyone in his crew to know all his special ingredients.

When the boys arrive, they see that a light is on in the back of the store. Georgio knocks on the glass front door. He sees a tall man, a little older and heavier than his Papa, come to unlock the door.

Wally sees the boys and quickly realizes they're too young to be insured by his insurance policy for the job. However, his storefront windows need cleaning badly and he doesn't want to waste his valuable time cleaning them. So, he quickly plans to give them "On the job work experience." He decides that he will allow them to wash his dirty double storefront windows and pay each of them $5.

"I'm Wally, this is my place of business. Has any of you ever washed a window? Raise your hand if you did."

No one raises a hand. "Okay, I'll show you how it's done. First, you need a bucket with water; a package of my special cleaning solution; a cloth to spread it on the glass; and a window wiper. Inside the building, you'll wipe on the solution from left to right. Then, outside the building you're going to wipe up and down. After that, you'll use the wiper and go down the window. Who can tell me why I want you to clean it this way?"

"Because that's the way you said it should be done, boss," says Edwardo.

"Can anyone else think of a reason why I want it done this way?"

"You can tell if you missed a spot on the window that needs to be cleaned from the outside, or the inside," says Georgio.

"That's the right answer… Okay, now each of you grab a pail and fill it with water. You'll find all the supplies are in the boxes in the backroom. After that, I'll take you to the windows where I'll be able to clock the speed of your work, but first, I must inspect each of your IDs." He then asked each of them to sign a waiver of liability. After all this is done, the boys follow Wally with the supplies through the store.

He leads them to the front windows. Wally knew each of them were too young to legally sign anything. However, his store front windows need cleaning badly, and he's too busy to do it. So, he's really glad to set them to work to clean his windows.

Wally pulls out his stopwatch to time their performance. He tells them "Work as fast as you can, men."

The phone rings in the rear of the store and Wally hands his stopwatch to Georgio to time the others at work while he goes to answer the phone.

Soon, a black-haired girl comes to the store carrying a small package. She asks, "Where's Wally?" Georgio replies, "Mr. Wally went to answer the phone, he'll be right back. Won't you please sit down and wait for him."

She doesn't tell the very handsome young man who spoke to her so politely that she's Wally's daughter. She was too enraptured with his good looks and nice manners. Then, she tries in vain to make eye-contact with the busy new employee, but he is too busy doing his job.

***

Wally comes to the doorway and sees his daughter. "Isabella," he calls, and then waves his arm for her to come into the back room.

"Daddy, when did you hire that polite fellow?"

"I didn't. He and the others are too young for my insurance policy to insure them to work for me. So, I put them to work on my dirty storefront windows. I'll give them each five bucks and the experience of how to wash a window."

"Too bad" she says, "That one seems to take his work very seriously."

"Isabella, why have you come here this morning?"

"You forgot to take your lunch again. I'm worried about you, Papa, you've been forgetting to do a lot of stuff lately. Maybe you need someone around to remind you... like an assistant maybe?"

"Isabella, when I forget my lunch, I get to see more of you, Sweetie, but you gave me an idea. Maybe, I should hire that polite boy to stay in the office to mix my cleanser solution, take calls, pay the bills, and make out the checks. All that office work wastes too much of my valuable time... when I could be out cleaning windows and making money."

After he says that, she hugs him and says, "Daddy, you're such a clever man."

Unbeknownst to Isabella, Georgio saw her hug Wally and he becomes upset because he assumes she's using her good looks to throw herself at a rich old man to get herself ahead in the world.

After she leaves, Georgio respects Mr. Wally for not responding to her embrace. Then, he wonders why he should even care about that girl… but he does. In fact, Georgio wants to run after her and scold her for trying to throw herself at the old man. He admires Mr. Wally for sending her away quickly.

When the boys are finished cleaning the windows, Wally hands each of them $5 and says, "I'll call you if I need you."

However, Georgio protests, "My mother makes twelve dollars an hour for cleaning apartments. We're men and want a man's wages for the work we do here."

"Hmm…. You're a polite, yet savvy young man. I can use a fellow like you to work for me in the store starting when your school year ends from 9:00 AM to 3:00 PM." Then, Wally gives each of them a $10 bill. Georgio's friends are pleased that he spoke up and don't begrudge him being offered a job to work at Wally's store this summer.

***

Georgio weighs out each of the ingredients for Mr. Wally's special window wash as he'd been instructed. He then seals it in a plastic bag and places it into one of the boxes at the rear wall of the store next to the cleaning pails he'd scrubbed. Each of the boxes is designed to hold fifty of these plastic bags.

The work crews enter for fresh supplies every morning… they return their used pails and take a clean pail. After that, they collect as many plastic formula bags as needed; depending on the number of windows of each building job that is assigned to them to be done that day.

Wally is pleased Georgio has managed to fill all the boxes at the rear wall each day. It's a tedious task, but it has to be done and he's glad that he's no longer the one who's doing it.

He congratulates himself for hiring this smart and hardworking kid. It has enabled him to use more of his time to clean windows and make more money. He's already cut the usual six weeks visits to five weeks.

***

After dinner, Wally mentions to Isabella how pleased he was with the polite boy that she recommended to him. Isabella then asks him for the work sheets of his employees to make out their paychecks.

It is then that Wally realizes he had forgotten to tell Georgio about making them out. "Isabella, when I showed that boy what he needed to do, I forgot all about the work sheets."

"Baby doll, I want you to give each man the same amount of money that he got last month. Tomorrow, you go to the shop and show Georgio how to fill out those worksheets."

"All right, Papa."

Chapter 13

It was another scorching, hot day in July in Manhattan. Georgio had removed his shirt while he worked in the sweltering heat of the shop without an air conditioner or fan. He listened to music on his radio while he worked and didn't hear the bell ring on the door when Isabella entered.

As soon as he notices her in the room, he removes his ear plugs, switches off the radio, and puts his shirt on. "I'm Isabella. I've come to show you how to make the work sheets for the men."

Georgio says in a contemptuous tone of voice, "So, you did get yourself a job with Mr. Wally after all?"

She looks at him with a puzzled expression and says, "Wally is my father and I do all I can to help him."

Georgio apologizes, "Oh, I'm sorry… I'm so sorry... I didn't know Wally is your father," he says and blushes while buttoning his shirt...I thought..."

"What did you think?" she asked him.

"Forgive me...I happened to see you kiss the old man and then he sent you away. It seemed to me that you had tried to throw yourself at a rich old man to advance yourself... and he'd told you to leave."

Since Isabella has a crush on Georgio, she knows it would be foolish of her to be angry with him and spoil a relationship even before it got started... therefore she laughs and says, "The fact that you care what becomes of me makes me realize you care about me… and what becomes of me. That's very sweet, Georgio. Thank you."

After telling him that, she walks over and kisses him on the cheek and they shake hands. She's glad to use this incident to become better friends with Georgio.

"You're not familiar with this neighborhood yet. I can show you around, it's almost your lunchtime."

He hesitates and says, "I must finish what I start to do first, Isabella. You came here to show me additional work that your father wants me to do?"

She replies "Yes, that's right."

"Additional work means Mr. Wally is satisfied with my work and he thinks I can do more to help him?"

"Yes, that's right."

"Well... additional work should bring with it an increase in my pay. Let me see what you brought with you, Isabella."

***

At the dinner table, Isabella says, "Daddy, Georgio is a hard worker. He's already filled all the boxes in the store. I showed him how you wanted him to make out the work forms and he suggested a space should be added to indicate how many boxed cleaning packets each man is given."

"Hmm... I knew he was a savvy kid right away. If I know how many boxes are used exactly then I can determine which workers are honest or waste my materials; or if a fellow took too much time to do the building assigned to him to do the job."

"Daddy, Georgio said that he's glad you like the job he's doing for you and since you realize you need him to do more, he asks for a raise in pay."

"What?" Wally shrieked... But he soon calms down and says, "That young rascal has the makings of a darn good politician," he laughs.

"Papa, I like him, too. Are you going to give him a raise?"

"Yes, I think I should. I'm already making more money because I hired him. Isabella, I want you to find out when that boy will graduate. A savvy young man can be a useful asset to any business."

"Daddy, it's very hot in your store. If you want to keep Georgio thinking sharp, it might be a good idea to put in an air conditioner."

"It's a legitimate business expense, Isabella. Call up and have one installed tomorrow."

"Yes, Papa. I will."

Chapter 14

Georgio was pleased to see an air conditioner being installed in the store the next day. He wonders if it's a substitute for the increase in pay that he was hoping to get.

The following day, Isabella enters the store to show Georgio the revised worksheet. He's very pleased to hear her say he'll be getting an increase in pay.

He asks Isabella to go out to lunch with him to help him celebrate, and she agrees. After walking up the street, they pause on the corner... Georgio buys two hot dogs from the street vendor.

Georgio asks what she wants on her hot dog. "Everything please," she replies. Isabella had been looking forward to dining at her favorite restaurant two blocks further up, but she realizes she's been expecting more from this young man than he can afford. So, she smiles sweetly as she accepts the frankfurter and thanks him for it.

***

A week later, Isabella comes to the store after her morning classes at summer school with her books and a brown paper lunch bag. She says, "Georgio, may I ask a favor of you?"

"Whatever it is, Isabella, my answer is yes. I can deny you nothing."

She's pleased and smiles at him and says, "I've this problem. I believe to waste food is a sin. I keep telling my mother I want to lose a few pounds, but she insists on packing lunches that are far too much for me to eat. Please, Georgio, will you share my lunch with me?"

"What've you brought in that bag, Isabella?"

"I'll show you."

She reaches into the bag and pulls out an enormous meatloaf sandwich.

He says, "It looks and smells delicious. I'll be glad to share it with you. I think we should have sodas to go with it. Is a coke okay with you, Isabella?"

She smiles and nods. He runs to the corner to purchase two cokes from the street vendor.

***

After he finishes his sandwich, Georgio says, "Isabella, your mother is a marvelous cook. I've never tasted anything this delicious."

"Yes, I'm glad she taught me how to cook from the time when I was a little girl."

"You mean to tell me you're beautiful and you can cook this good, too."

She giggles and asks, "Do you really think I'm beautiful?"

He replies, "Isabella, when I first saw you, my heart skipped a beat. I asked you to sit and wait with me so I could look at you for a longer time."

"Oh, Georgio, I confess, I didn't tell you who I was when I walked in because I wanted to sit and look at you, too. I like the way you speak to me. You make me feel like I'm important."

"My mother is a beautiful woman, too. However, she was brought up in a wealthy home and she doesn't know how to cook anything but rice. She was taught to manage and train the household staff, decorate, and have good manners."

"We're both blessed children, Georgio."

"Yes, you're right. Thank you for the wonderful lunch, I need to get back to work or your father will be disappointed. Good afternoon, Isabella. Maybe we can do this again soon."

Isabella didn't want to go, but she understood he'd asked her to leave… but in the nicest way she'd ever heard. So she replies, "Goodbye for now, Georgio."

Chapter 15

"What's the matter, Isabella? Why have you been moping around? What's wrong, sweetheart?"

"Mama, there's a boy I like and I think he likes me... but he doesn't even try to flirt with me."

"Is this that young man who works for your dad that you're talking about?"

"Yes, Mama" she sighs and rests her head on her mother's shoulder."

Sophia strokes her daughter's hair and says, "Isabella, your daddy is this boy's employer. Maybe he's just being careful. He doesn't want to get fired or mislead you. I think he must be a very smart boy. I'd like to meet him. Why don't you ask him to come to dinner?"

"Oh, Mama, that's a great idea. Then he won't be able to use his job as an excuse for not paying attention to me. Georgio already knows that you're a very good cook. He loved your meatloaf sandwich. I took one with me for him to share at lunch time."

"You invite Georgio to come eat with us on Saturday. It sounds to me like this young man takes pride in his appearance. He'll want time to freshen up, otherwise, I'd say Friday night would be good."

"May I offer him a choice?"

"That's a good idea, Isabella."

***

That night at dinner, Wally complimented his wife on her cooking. Then he said, "Isabella, it's near the end of the month. Pick up the worksheets from Georgio after school tomorrow please.

"Yes, Papa. I'll be cramming for my finals next week."

"I'm going to miss that boy," said Wally.

"Are you going to fire him, daddy?"

"No, he'll be graduating from high school."

"Will you hire him again next year?"

"Next year, he may be going after a better job. He'll be a graduate."

"However, if Georgio goes on to college, he may need a part time or summer job, Daddy."

Wally says, "Honestly, Isabella, I'd hire him in a flash. He's an experienced worker now and will be a graduate, too."

***

From his desk, Georgio looks up and smiles as Isabella enters.

"I like your new hair comb, Isabella. It's very becoming."

"I'm glad you like it, Georgio. I came here today to pick up the worksheets and to invite you to dinner."

"Where?"

"At my house Friday or Saturday night?"

"I'll need to check something and then I'll let you know."

"When?"

"There's something I must do, Isabella, before I can give you my answer. Here are the work sheets you asked me for... I thank you for your invitation, Isabella. Goodbye for now."

She was perplexed and wondered why he was being mysterious about accepting her dinner invitation. So, Isabella discusses it with her mother. Both women were puzzled.

Sophia decides to make out a menu for Friday night featuring fish and one for Saturday featuring lasagna. After that, she gave this information to Isabella to pass along to Georgio.

***

Wally enters the store while Georgio is helping one of the workers carry out several boxes that he needs to complete his work order. When he's finished, Georgio walks over to Wally and says, "Senor Wally, I was asked by a member of your family to come to dinner at your house, but I will not accept until I have your permission to come to your home."

No one before had ever asked Wally for his permission. He was suddenly impressed with his own importance as the master of his home for the first time in his life. After he savors this new feeling for a few moments, he thrusts out his hand to shake Georgio's while saying, "You're welcome to come to my home anytime."

Georgio smiles and shakes his hand. "Thank you, Senor Wally." Then he asks, "Please tell me, Senor Wally, what is Lasagna?"

Chapter 16

Isabella came to the store on Friday to share her lunch with Georgio. He was glad to see her and she smiled broadly as he seated her. "Isabella," he starts to explain, "I can now accept your dinner invitation for this Saturday night. It was necessary for me to get your father's permission first before accepting your invitation."

"Oh... that was the reason you made me wait. I thought you didn't like me enough or there was someone else that you were more interested in. So, you weren't trying to avoid hurting my feelings."

Georgio puts his pen down and says, "Isabella, the first time I saw you, my heart skipped a beat. There's no one else that I'm more interested in."

A glow of happiness sweeps over Isabella's face and she confesses, "I wanted to stay and look at you, too, but you kept avoiding my eye contact. Whenever I come to the store, you don't seem to want me to linger awhile and get to know you. You always rush me out."

"I'm employed here, Isabella. Let's eat, my lunch break is nearly over."

***

"Mama, you're so clever to have invited Georgio here to dinner. He told me that he had to ask Daddy for his permission before he would agree to come to our home."

Sophia says, "What refined manners that young man has."

"Georgio told me his mother was born into a very wealthy family. She never learned to cook, but was taught to give household orders, have good manners, and to decorate."

"It sounds to me like she was taught to be an elegant lady. I'll make a special dessert for her."

***

Maria asks, "Georgio, can you see your reflection in your shoes yet?"

He laughs and says, "Just about, Mama." He lays out his clothes carefully on the bed and takes a shower. He shaves before he gets dressed.

"Mama, I won't be here for dinner, I've been invited to a friend's house for dinner tonight."

"Will you bring her flowers or wine, Georgio?"

"I didn't know I was supposed to bring anything, Mama."

"It's customary to bring a small gift to the table of your host."

"Is a box of candy okay?"

"A box of nice chocolates will be fine, son. In the future, let me know when you have a dinner invitation a few days in advance so Papa and I will have time to make other plans if you won't be here and I won't buy more groceries than what is necessary."

"I'm sorry I didn't think to tell you sooner, Mama. I'll be sure to tell you in the future. Please forgive me." He gives her a kiss on the cheek.

"So where will you be eating dinner tonight?"

"I'm having dinner at my employer's home. His daughter asked me to come and I got his permission before I accepted the invitation."

"Very good and quite correct. I'm proud of you, son. She should come with a large dowry."

"Mama... a dowry? I'm just having dinner there. What're you talking about? I'm too young to get married. I haven't even finished high school. I've never even kissed her."

"Georgio, do you want to kiss her?"

"I did... but now I'm not so sure I will... She's a school kid like me, Mama."

"You're right, Georgio. This is only a dinner. Perhaps, I overreacted to my young son having some fun at his girlfriend's home. It's not like you're a graduate and have a job and you aren't looking for a wife yet."

"That's right, Mama. Now you understand what is to happen tonight."

"Have a good time, son."

Chapter 17

With a box of mixed chocolates tucked under his arm, Georgio rang the doorbell of Wally's home. Sophia answered the door and smiled at the young man. He is even more handsome than she'd thought he'd be. She also thinks, this fellow and my Isabella would make the most beautiful grandchildren in the entire family. All of my sisters would be jealous of me. What a shame that he's not an Italian boy.

Georgio presents her with the box of chocolates and says, "I've never eaten lasagna before. I'm looking forward to eating yours tonight."

"My wife makes the best Italian food in the city," says Wally while patting his stomach...

"You're lucky to be here."

"Thank you again for permission to come to your home, Mr. Wally." Sophia strikes the dinner chime and asks for everyone to be seated at the table while she and Isabella serve dinner.

***

After the delicious-looking and wonderful smelling food was placed on his plate, Georgio awaits the women to be seated and asks Wally if he might say grace tonight.

Wally is a little embarrassed not to have said it already and quickly gives his permission to Georgio. Sophia was very impressed with this boy and was sorry that he wasn't born Italian.

***

When dinner ends, the dishes are cleared and placed in the dishwasher. A deck of cards is brought to the table and they play "Hearts." Georgio was glad that he was familiar with this game. He and his parents played it often.

Sophia was able to "Shoot the moon" twice and was very pleased with herself. Afterward, she walked into the kitchen and came back with a box for Georgio to take home with him. He understood it was time for him to leave and said, "Thank you for the delicious food. I really enjoyed the evening with all of you."

Isabella says, "It's time for me to walk my dog. I'll walk with you to the train station, Georgio."

***

"Wally sat down on his leather club chair and lit his pipe. Sophia brought him a towel and a large container of warm water to soak his feet in.

"What a shame Georgio isn't an Italian boy."

"Sophia, what makes you say that?"

"Because he would be a perfect fit for our Isabella."

"Do you think he's interested in Isabella?"

"I can't be sure if he's interested in her or not, but I know that she really likes him."

"Sophia, they're just school kids. He's a nice boy and does his job well, but I doubt anything will come of it. I'd really like it if Georgio was interested in her, then I could be sure he'd come back to work for me after he graduates."

"Che sera sera" she says and kisses her husband goodnight. She turns on the television set in the living room and gives him the remote before going upstairs to bed.

***

Outside the house, Isabella takes hold of his arm and asks, "Did you have a good time, Georgio?"

"Yes, I did, your mother's a marvelous cook. I never knew a noodle could taste so good."

They pause while the dog sniffs the fire hydrant. Isabella quickly stands on tiptoe and kisses him... "Goodnight," she says, "I'm glad you came."

Putting the box down, he takes her in his arms and kisses her. Georgio really likes the taste of her lips and kisses her again. She puts her arms around his neck and kisses him back. Taking his hand, she guides him to the nearby park to sit, kiss, and hug some more.

***

Unbeknownst to them, a new neighbor is sitting on a bench in the distance. With lustful wonton eyes, he decides to relieve himself while he excitedly watches them kiss and fondle one another.

They stop abruptly and he is suddenly left with no alternative to his unbearable loneliness. Seeing them leave the bench, he quickly stands up and follows after them.

Under a park light, he recognizes the lusty female is a church member's daughter. He's never seen the handsome boy that she's been sinfully kissing. He follows them to the subway station and continues to watch them.

"Will you come again?" Isabella asks.

"Anytime you say, Isabella" He covers her face with more kisses.

"Call me when you get home."

"Give me your number and I'll call you every night before I go to sleep."

***

The man sees the boy leaving the sinful girl to enter the subway. Now she is alone. His eyes grow large as he furtively looks both ways to see if anyone is on the street. There are none present. He quickly walks over to the girl and asks if he can pet her dog.

Without waiting for her reply, he swiftly bends down, snatches up the dog, and places it under his arm. He starts to run towards the park with it.

Isabella is surprised and upset by his actions. She screams, "Stop! Put my dog down!" Frantically, she tugs at its leash while running after the man.

The dog squirms to free itself and tries to bite the man. They enter the darkness of the deserted park.

The man reaches into his pocket and adroitly pulls out his switchblade with a routine like precision. He knows exactly how to end any resistance to his plan to fulfill his desire.

The dog howls in pain as he plunges his knife into her dog. Isabella is horrified to see him do this and watches helplessly. After dropping her dog, he menacingly advances towards her.

***

When Georgio arrives home, he puts the box in the refrigerator. He hums a tune as he lays out his clothes for church and gets ready for bed.

He hears his parents come home and enter the kitchen for their bedtime snack. Georgio pulls on his robe and slippers and goes to say goodnight.

He sees them sitting at the table waiting for the coffee to percolate. They'd already opened the box and are waiting to try the Tiramisu dessert he brought home.

Georgio hoped the box he was given held some leftover Lasagna that he'd enjoyed so much at dinner, but was glad to see his folks were happy with the fancy dessert Sophia had made for him to take home.

His parents ask him to join them, and he pulls out a kitchen chair and sits waiting with them. Carlos asks, "What did they serve you for dinner?"

"Wally's wife made a noodle and meat dish called lasagna. It was very different from what we eat, but very tasty. Sophia really liked the chocolates, Mama. Thanks for telling me to bring a gift with me."

"What did you do after dinner?"

"We played 'Hearts.'"

"So, they eat differently yet enjoy the same game we play, eh?"

"Yes, Papa."

"You had a good time, son?" asked Maria.

Georgio nods his head.

"Did you kiss her yet?" Georgio blushes.

"A gentleman doesn't kiss and tell, Maria. Papa says. Right, son?"

"May I use the phone? I promised I'd let them know I got home safely."

His dad nods. Georgio carries the phone into the bathroom. He is careful to close the door behind him.

Having memorized Isabella's number, he eagerly dials it.

The phone rings and continues to ring. Wally answers it. He's surprised to hear his voice say, "I've been waiting up for you, Isabella. Where are you?"

"It's Georgio. I'm calling to speak to Isabella. Isn't she there yet?"

"No, I thought she was still with you."

"No. Wally, I left her at the train station over an hour ago. I promised to call her before I went to bed."

"I must go look for my Isabella!"

Now worried, he drops the phone.

"Sophia! Wake up, Isabella isn't with Georgio."

"I'll look in her room," she calls down to him.

"Wally, she's not in there. Is she in the kitchen?"

"No, I already looked in there."

"Wally, the park isn't big, but it's very dark there. Get the flashlight! I always tell her to walk around the park," she sobbed. "Wally, the traffic cop goes to visit his girlfriend at the coffee shop when he gets off duty. So, go there and see if he'll help you look for Isabella. I'll meet you there as soon as I get dressed."

Chapter 18

After Sophia puts on her dress, she hurries to the coffee shop. The counter girl is standing in the doorway of the store when she arrives.

"Did my husband find your friend here?" asked Sophia.

"Yes, he and all the customers that were in the shop went to search for your daughter in the park."

Suddenly, they hear the whine of an ambulance scream as it passes by and enter the park. "Oh my God! My daughter's been hurt."

"You look faint."

The shopkeeper takes her arm and guides her to a seat at a table.

"Please sit down."

A bobbing Sophia is handed a handkerchief and offered water.

A few minutes later, a police officer enters and goes to sit beside the distressed looking woman.

"They took your daughter to the hospital. Your husband left with them in the ambulance. He told me that you'd be in here. I'll drive you home," said the experienced police officer.

"You'll need to get your purse and the insurance papers. Then, I'll take you to the hospital."

"Yes, thank you."

***

Sophia sees that an unfamiliar car is parked in her driveway. There're strangers sitting on her porch.

"I don't know those people on my porch," she tells the policeman.

"You stay in the car, I'll find out what they're doing here."

***

"Sophia, do you know a Mr. and Mrs. Lopez? They say their son, Georgio, was here tonight. He was worried after he kept getting a busy signal on the phone and his parents wanted to be sure Isabella is all right, so they borrowed a car and drove over here to find out."

Sophia gets out of the car and walks up the stairs to meet the people on her dark porch. She recognizes Georgio who's wearing a coat over his robe.

Maria says, "I'm going to the hospital now. I don't know how Isabella is." She starts to weep.

Carlos says, "Please let us drive you there. You're in no condition to drive on your own."

The police officer says, "That's a great idea."

He tells Carlos the address of the hospital and quickly leaves. Sophia goes inside to get her purse and takes the health files out of the cabinet with the insurance cards. Seeing the living room phone dangling at the side of her husband's club chair, she lifts the phone and hears a busy signal. She sighs. Sophia is relieved to know Georgio has told the truth.

***

At the hospital, they are appalled to see a very pale unconscious Isabella lying on a stretcher. She hadn't yet been admitted, but a doctor has attempted to stop the bleeding from her neck wound.

Sophia immediately places all the health cards and insurance policy on the intake nurse's desk. She patiently answers the questions that will enable her daughter to be admitted to the hospital.

She walks over to ask her husband for his wallet since the hospital also wants a credit card before Isabella can be admitted.

After all the paperwork is done for their unconscious daughter, she is wheeled into another area. She's given blood while they wait for a doctor to arrive.

The Lopez family silently drove home feeling sad and weary. They're all disappointed not to know the fate of Isabella.

***

The doctor comes to examine the young unconscious girl with a slit throat. Afterward, he tells the waiting parents, "Your daughter is a very lucky girl. With a wound like the one she received, the victim often dies before medical assistance can reach her. There's a very good chance that she'll survive."

"Let's go home and pray," says a tearful Sophia.

Chapter 19

It was early in the morning when the cab delivered the weary elderly couple to their home. After he pays the driver, Wally and Sophia see there's a trail of blood on the street leading to the path at the side of their home, they follow it.

They find Isabella's dog at the kitchen door. She's still breathing, but badly hurt and bloodied. The dog is in need of immediate attention by a vet.

Sophia searches for a box to put the dog in while Wally opens the garage and backs the car out. She puts the dog in the box and puts the box in the car.

"I'll take her right over to the animal hospital," he says before leaving.

Sophia decides to go inside and call the police to tell them they found Isabella's dog badly hurt but alive.

***

The following evening, the phone rings and Sophia hurries to answer it. She hears Georgio say, "I phoned the hospital, but all they would tell me is that Isabella's on the critical list. How's she doing?"

"The doctor thinks she has a good chance to survive because she was found before she lost too much blood."

"Thanks be to God," says Georgio.

"Her dog was at the kitchen door when we got home, Georgio. He was badly hurt. Wally took him over to the animal hospital. It's good that you called here last night and alerted us that Isabella hadn't come back home. Thank you. Finding her quickly saved her life. Call me tomorrow, maybe I'll be able to give you more news. Goodbye, Georgio."

***

Georgio was glad to hear that he'd helped Isabella in some way.

"What a terrible thing to have happened to a sweet girl," but finds it difficult to fall asleep that night.

He awoke too late in the morning. He hurriedly gathered his books and ran to school. Wanting to see Isabella, he considered the best day during his school week. "On Monday, new material was taught by his teachers. Tuesday, Wednesday, and Thursday were usually class drills to review what was taught on Monday. So, he planned to go over Monday's work on Tuesday and Wednesday, which would be enough time for him to ace the test on Friday. So, he decided Thursday to be the best day for him to visit her.

***

Wednesday night, Georgio phones the hospital and is told no visitors were being allowed to visit Isabella except her family. So, he phoned her house to ask her parents how she was doing.

He let the phone ring several times and was about to hang up when he heard the voice of Isabella's mother answer, "Hello."

"This is Georgio, I learned no one is allowed to see Isabella yet. I'd hoped to visit her tomorrow. How's she doing?""

"Meet me at the hospital at 1 o'clock tomorrow, Georgio. I think she would like to see you."

***

Georgio was prompt on his arrival. Sophia led the way to Isabella's room. He was shocked to see all the tubes that had been placed into Isabella. He went to her bedside, took her hand, and asked, "What's wrong with her, Sophia? Why is she still asleep?"

"The doctor said she was traumatized by her terrible experience and has escaped into a safer place."

"How will she know that she's safe now?"

"We're all waiting for Isabella to feel safe again. She won't swallow any food yet. They're feeding her through those tubes and are monitoring her other body functions with the wires."

"All these tubes must be terribly uncomfortable, Isabella must be suffering. How can she be happy about being alive when they're torturing her like this, Sophia?" He kissed Isabella's fingertip and called her name.

He turned to Sophia and said, "It's too quiet in this room, Isabella likes music. Can you bring her favorite records here and play them for her?"

"That's a good idea, Georgio. I'll bring her a record player and records next time I come."

"Which were her favorite television shows?"

"Yes, I see what you mean, Georgio. I'll have them bring a television set in today. I'm glad you came with me, you've made me feel more hopeful. Thank you for coming with me to see her."

"Goodbye, Sophia. May I call you to find out how Isabella is doing? By the way, how's her dog doing?"

"I don't know, my husband has been handling that problem. You can call me any night you'd like."

"I'm sure Isabella would like to know if her dog is all right."

***

After dinner, Georgio found out he was out of cigarettes and decided to go to the store to pick up a pack. On his way to the grocery store, he meets Edwardo walking his dog. They hadn't seen one another for some time and Georgio tells him about the stabbing.

Edwardo was sorry to hear about it. He asked Georgio if it was a spade knifing because Wally had hired a member of a rival gang to work for him?

Had her stabbing been gang related? Georgio suddenly feels responsible and guilty, recalling Josh had said "Spades slash throats."

It made Edwardo's question a plausible explanation for Isabella's throat being slashed. This made Georgio feel he was therefore at fault in some way.

It upset Georgio to think he might be responsible for provoking this awful crime against Isabella that very nearly cost her life.

He finds it difficult to listen to the rest of Eduardo's news about the arrest and conviction of "Corto" for stealing spray paint despite the fact no spray cans were found in his possession when he was arrested.

The paint store owner had picked him out of a line up. He'd been high and forgot to check the location of the camera. It angered Georgio to hear Corto had been high and acted carelessly. He believed Josh when he said he wouldn't deal with drugs. He'd broken his word and now Corto was convicted and sentenced because of it. Who would be next because of his leader's deceit and poor judgment?

***

Feelings of guilt about the stabbing were uncomfortable for Georgio, so he decided the only way to rid himself of these gnawing feelings of guilt was to ask Mr. Wally if he'd been threatened because he'd hired a Latino to work for him.

***

After dinner, Georgio called Mr. Wally at home. As soon as he heard a "Hello," he said, "Mr. Wally, I saw Isabella at the hospital last week. How's she doing now?"

"She still hasn't regained consciousness yet. The doctor said he thinks she'll pull out of her coma soon."

"I'm relieved to hear her recovery is near."

"Yes."

"Mr. Wally, did anyone object to me working for you?"

"No, Georgio. In fact, I was hoping you'd come back to work for me after you graduate, if you're not going to college."

"I haven't decided yet, Mr. Wally. Thank you for your confidence in me. I'm glad to hear that Isabella is showing some improvement. Goodnight."

Georgio sighed and was relieved to learn Isabella was improving and that it was not because of him that she'd been stabbed. Without the distraction of a burden of guilt, he was able to concentrate better on his schoolwork afterwards.

***

Georgio was called to the Guidance Counselor's office shortly after he arrived at school the following day. Awaiting his turn, he wondered why he'd been called here today. He was soon called into Mr. Smith's office. Mr. Smith rose and congratulated Georgio on passing a battery of tests that had been given last month for the four-year college scholarship.

Georgio smiled after a moment of being stunned by the good news. He was then asked if he could afford to attend college without a scholarship.

"No, sir. I'm not even sure that I can go with a scholarship."

"Thank you for your frankness, Georgio."

***

After dinner, Georgio considers whether or not he should share the news of his visit to Mr. Smith's office with his parents. He didn't think that they could afford for him to go, yet he decides it would please them to know that the school considered him "college material." Carlos puts down his newspaper and gets up to shake his hand and hug him. Maria stopped washing the dishes, dried her hands, and applauded. She hurries to hug and kiss him.

Georgio is amazed by their reaction to his news. It seems to him that they actually do want him to go to college.

"Son, you'll be the first in our family to go to college," said his father.

"Carlos, what're you talking about? He'll be the first to go to college in this entire neighborhood. I can hardly wait to tell the ladies in my sewing circle."

Georgio was surprised by their reaction and stunned by the realization that he would be able to go to college. He found it hard to believe that his parents weren't just pleased with the fact that he was smart enough to go to college.

They're actually looking forward to me going to college. He looked at their happy, loving faces, and tears came into his eyes.

"You mean I can go? I didn't think we could afford for me to go to college."

"Son, this is the hope we shared when we came to this country. Giving you the freedom to get an education and enable you to choose whatever you want to be in this great country can happen."

"I'm not sure I know what I want to be yet. I've heard computer programmers make a lot of money, Then I could pay you back quickly and contribute to the household."

***

In the school hallway the following day, Edwardo tells Georgio that Josh wants him to show up tonight.

"It's been too long since you've come to a gang meeting." Georgio was surprised that Josh hadn't just forgotten about him.

Edwardo says, "See you tonight."

***

Georgio reflects on the reason why Josh might want him to come tonight. Is it to congratulate me about the college scholarship or something else? He recalled the pledge he'd made when he'd joined: "Once you're a member of this gang, you can never stop being a member."

After recalling that, he remembers participating in the beating of a brother who hadn't been around to take part in the activities of the gang for some time. Hmm... he wondered uneasily, What does Josh have in mind for me tonight?

***

That night, there was no moon and it was foggy. Georgio walked through the haze to meet Josh and the other guys under the lamppost. He continues to wonder, What does Josh have in mind for me tonight. Was he angry because I haven't been participating in the gang's activities? Had he heard about me going to college? Was he jealous of me? He remembers the pain of being beaten up.

"Oh Lord, I'm scared, I need your protection badly now. Please guide me!"

Georgio recalls that he still owes Josh for the cab fare to see Mr. Wally. He stops walking and digs out the money from his pants pocket sufficient enough to repay him.

As Georgio approaches the corner, he sees the silent boys under the lamp light. The quiet scene appears ominous to him and he's uneasy. No one greeted him. Georgio says to the silent group, "Hi fellas."

The hostility he senses was thicker than the fog. Georgio suddenly thought to say, "The sentence Corto got for a misdemeanor upset me, fellas. I've been busy studying to try to get into college. I want to become a lawyer, then you guys will be able to count on me to defend you in court. I haven't had time to come here before now. I don't want anyone else to get an inferior public defender like the one the court appointed to defend our bro, Corto."

Georgio saw the guys weren't acting any friendlier toward him. So, he silently prayed and said, "Fellas, you'll be glad to hear that I got a scholarship and I will be going to college to study law."

"You'll be a good lawyer, Georgio," says Josh.

"I'm glad we'll be able to count on you to defend us in the future."

Josh reaches for his hand to shake.

"That's great news. Ain't that right fellas."

He shakes his and says, "We're tight."

The boys nodded and one by one shook Georgio's hand. Suddenly, it started to rain and the group quickly dispersed under the shelter of some nearby trees.

Josh says, "Our gang can use a lawyer. I'm glad you're thinking of our future, Georgio. It's good we didn't need to remind you that you belong with us. I think you'll make a very good lawyer."

Georgio says, "Thanks for saying that, Josh. Your approval of what I do means a lot to me. Here's the money I loaned from you to go to that job interview, thanks for lending it to me."

Josh took the money and pocketed the cash without any comment. Then, slapping him on the back, he says, "Goodnight, my very smart future lawyer."

Georgio confronts Josh by saying, "Hey, I thought we agreed we wouldn't use maryjuana. So, how come Corto was high when he got busted?"

Josh replies, "I kept the agreement that we wouldn't use it, but I didn't say I wouldn't be a candyman to those who wanted to buy it."

"Josh, you look so thin to me. Are you sick or something?"

"Nah. Losing weight is easy when you use heroin."

A lightning bolt streaks across the sky above their heads with a crack of thunder and the rain pours down through the trees. Each of them pulls his jacket over his head and runs homeward.

Georgio was glad that he'd been able to change Josh's plan for him tonight. He was relieved that he hadn't been punished by his "brothers" for neglecting them and proud of himself for being able to convince Josh that he'd be an asset to the gang by going to college and becoming a lawyer. However, in the doorway of his home, he looks up and says, "Thanks Lord, for guiding me out of trouble with my gang. The idea of becoming a lawyer is a good one, but I'm not looking forward to telling my parents that I've changed my mind about my career choice and won't be making a lot of money. I did want to repay them for my college education as soon as possible, but now it will take me longer.

Should I confess to them that I'm in a gang and needed the excuse of becoming a lawyer to escape being beaten up by them? Georgio was in a quandary and didn't like how it made him feel.

So, he decided to act immediately and tell his parents as quickly as possible why he had to change his career.

His parents were seated at the table drinking coffee when he entered the apartment. Maria quickly handed him a towel and then poured him a hot cup of coffee.

"Sit with us," said Carlos.

Georgio took a seat at the table with them.

He said, "I'm grateful for this opportunity to go to college."

He was now hoping to convince them that just making money wasn't as important as being of help to their Latino community. Getting justice and being treated fairly under the law is more important than money. He felt certain that if he was able to satisfy his new decision with both groups that comprised his life, it would solve his dilemma. That would be a miracle.

It would mean that becoming a lawyer was always intended by God's Hand. This mystery of the Lord needed to be solved.

So, before Georgio went to bed, he told his dad of his revised decision. He was amazed to hear Carlos say, "Son, I'm so proud of you. You've thought about it and have now chosen a profession not to just make money and become rich, but to be of help to our friends and neighbors. I want everyone to prosper in this great country and be fairly protected under the laws here."

***

Before he fell asleep, Georgio recalled how he first decided to join a gang, continually being picked on by school, and neighborhood bullies. It wasn't fair. That fear of being beaten up had caused him to join a gang for his safety.

Now it was the fear of them that had caused him to say, "I want to become a lawyer. Am I being guided to make better choices for my life now by my Creator?

Is being of service to others more important than just how much money one can make? Is it only money that makes a person rich?"

Chapter 20

At school the following day, Georgio hurried to see Mr. Smith to accept the scholarship offer. Fortunately, Mr. Smith hadn't had the opportunity to notify the runner up of a scholarship space available to him, thus Georgio was able to claim it without any difficulty. With the matter now taken care of, he hurried to his classroom.

***

Georgio phoned Isabella's home. The phone was picked up before the second ring and a voice said "Hello," but Georgio didn't recognize this new voice of Isabella.

He said, "This is a friend of Isabella, please tell her that Georgio called."

"Wait Georgio! It's me, Isabella. My voice doesn't sound the same since I got hurt."

"I can hear you fine, Isabella. I'm glad you're recovering. We were all very worried about you. I called to share some good news with you. "

"Oh yes. I'd like that. When do you want to come over to see me?"

"I have some free time this evening if that's alright with you?"

"Oh yes. Shall I ask Mama to set a place for you at dinner?"

"No, I promised my mother to give her advance notice whenever I wouldn't be having dinner at home."

He glanced at his reflection in the window when he hung up and saw that he looked relieved to have made that promise. After that, he hurried to take the train to Isabella's station.

***

Georgio no longer felt guilty about what had happened to her. He didn't want to be involved with any girl right now. He was going to go to college and would be meeting new people and studying hard. That was now uppermost in his mind.

He just wanted Isabella's meeting today to be a casual visit to a recovering sick friend.

***

Getting off the train, Georgio noticed the florist shop on the station was open and decided to buy Isabella flowers. He entered the store and the eager owner offered him a good deal on red roses for his girlfriend.

"She's not my girlfriend, just a friend. When my dad gives my mother red roses, it's because they speak, "The language of love" he told me.

"What about carnations?"

"No, mom says they're for sick people and she's not sick anymore."

"Look around, young man, and tell me what you want."

It smelled nice in the store. Georgio wanted to give her a "It's good to see you back home" flowers. Then he spotted a bunch of daisies behind a plant.

"That's what I want," he said. "Fine, I'll wrap them up for you."

Georgio paid the man what he asked and was pleased with his choice.

***

He was glad Isabella's mother answered the door after he pressed the doorbell. They shook hands and she took the flowers to put in water for Isabella's room.

He waited until she returned then followed her up the stairs to visit his friend.

Isabella had decided to see Georgio in her room where it would be more private. She was hoping that he would kiss her and tell her how much he loved her Instead, she was surprised to hear him say that he belonged to a gang when he confessed his fear that he'd felt unnecessarily guilty for her stabbing.

Isabella was very disappointed to learn that it wasn't feelings for her, but guilt that had made him so attentive to her. She listened to how he'd cleverly talked his gang out of beating him up.

"I'm glad you decided to become a lawyer, Georgio. You learn quickly and will probably be a fine lawyer."

"Your father said he's willing to hire me back for the summer until school starts."

However, Isabella now no longer wants him to be as available to her if he isn't going to return her feelings of love.

"Georgio, I know you need to work, but shouldn't you try to get a job at a law office first?" she suggests.

"Caramba! That's a great idea. It never occurred to me to try to find work in a law office. It's great that I have a smart friend like you. Goodnight, Isabella. I'll call you and let you know if I am able to get a job at a law office. Thanks for the great idea."

"Goodnight, Georgio, and thank you for the flowers."

***

Georgio was glad that he'd gone to see Isabella and whistled a happy tune all the way to the train station. It was necessary for him to stand all the way home, but he didn't mind. The idea of working at a law firm was a good one he thought.

As soon as he got off the train, Georgio hurried over to the telephone booth on the station platform.

He opened the classified phonebook in the booth and turned the alphabetized pages to "L." He searched for "Lawyers."

Georgio was surprised to see that there were pages and pages of them listed in the directory. This is another challenge for me to overcome. So, Georgio closed his eyes, prayed, and then let his fingers lead him to a law firm in the book.

He called the phone number his finger guided him to: John Gilbert & Mario Fisherkelly.

The voice of the man who answered the phone sounded friendly to Georgio. He explained to him why he was calling.

"I must say, this is a novel approach to ask for a job. You must be a creative and smart fellow. We can use a man who thinks out of the box in our office. Georgio, come see us tomorrow morning at 9 o'clock and bring black coffee with you."

***

As soon as Georgio got home, he told his parents about the suggestion Isabella had made to him and the outcome, a job interview.

"That girl is lucky for you," said his mother.

"Where is this law firm located?" asked Papa.

"It's an office in the Fisher building downtown, Papa.

"They'll probably expect you to wear a suit and tie each day, son, and you only have one suit."

"That's okay, Papa. He knows it's my first job and I need to work to help pay for my education."

"Yes, that's right. It's good that you told him the truth."

"Papa, I feel I'm being guided in my life now because I'll be able to do good for our people when I become a lawyer."

"We agree with you, son. You're a lucky young man. Let's all join hands now and thank our Lord for His blessings of kindness and wisdom."

"Papa, is it only when I'm afraid that I will be guided?"

"Son, I believe we're all guided each day by opportunities that present themselves. It's up to us to choose to act upon them or not. After we've exhausted what we thought we know and out of our own way, then we are more likely to receive His guidance. If no idea comes right away, then the answer is to wait. Prayers aren't always answered in our time, son. It's in his time and not ours."

Chapter 21

Before going to sleep, Georgio told his mother more about the job he might be getting at the law firm and mentioned that he'd been asked to bring black coffee.

In the morning, he was delighted to find a thermos of black coffee Mama had brewed awaiting him on the kitchen table and her note wishing him good luck.

***

The train wasn't crowded when Georgio took a seat. He carried the thermos tucked under his arm. When the train finally arrives at his stop, he struggles through the crowded car before the door closes. He learns that the address he seeks is in this building above the train station. All he needs to do is to get into the elevator. In bad weather, it'll be ideal to be this close to my station.

***

Georgio arrives at 8:51, but finds the door is locked, so he knocks. Soon, a young man came to the door who Georgio thinks is not much older than himself. "Can I help you?"

"Hello, I'm Georgio. I've brought the coffee."

The young man says, "I'm Mario Fisherkelly. My partner, John Gilbert, told me to expect you."

"Nice to meet you, Mr. Fisherkelly. May I pour you a cup of coffee?"

"Okay, come into my office."

Georgio follows the man past an unmanned reception desk stacked with unopened letters and many unopened boxes on the floor along the blank wall to his office.

In his neat office, Georgio sees many books lining the shelves and many documents hung on the walls. A long black leather couch has a pillow and a neatly folded blanket on it. Through the open door to the bathroom, Georgio sees shaving tools laying on the sink. Mr. Fisherkelly takes a seat behind the desk. Meanwhile, Georgio goes into the bathroom and fetches three cups he noticed in there and brings them to the desk.

Georgio senses this man is uncomfortable about something while he squirms in his chair. Calmly, he asks, "May I pour you a cup of coffee, sir?"

The man nods and he pours the steaming brew into a cup and offers it to him. Mario accepts the cup and takes a sip. He clears his throat as if to deliver bad news to Georgio. However, after the first sip, he takes another, and another.

"What kind of coffee is this? I've never tasted a coffee this good before."

"Mama's family grew coffee plants. She knows all about how to make good coffee."

Mario flips a button on his desk and says, "John please come in here before I drink all the coffee Georgio brought."

He was thinking, John asked this boy to come here. Why should I have the unpleasant task of firing him? Then, Mario refreshed his cup and sat back in his chair, thinking... Maybe it would be a good idea to hire someone to help us set up our new office. If this young man can type, we could hire him as our receptionist. He's a very nice looking young man, too.

***

John Gilbert entered the room. Georgio thought he looked like a very kind man. He was much older than his father.

"John, have a cup of this coffee Georgio brought here this morning." Georgio pours him a cup.

John takes a few sips and says, "I told you Georgio was out of the box. This may be the best cup of coffee I've ever tasted. Which brand of coffee is this, Georgio?"

"My mother brewed it this morning. I'm not sure what brand she buys, sir."

"Georgio, the boxes in the other room need to be unpacked. Please see to them while I discuss something important with my associate."

"Yes, sir."

***

Georgio leaves the room and is worried. He'd sensed Mr. Fisherkelly was going to fire him before he even began to work here. So, Georgio prays and asks God for His help to get him a job at this office.

He walks over to open one of the boxes. In it are lots of framed photos of the two lawyers shaking hands with some people Georgio read about in the newspaper. He assumes they're satisfied clients. He thinks both lawyers would like to see them mounted on the walls of the reception area. He sees there's a hammer and nails in the box, but no measuring tape.

Georgio quickly removes his belt and uses it to measure where to place each nail on the wall. Fortunately, all the photos and awards were in the same sized frame. After he hammers the nails in, Georgio lays out the photos and awards on the floor to arrange them. After he's satisfied with his arrangement of them, he hangs the photos and awards. Hanging up the last framed photo, the two men appear to tell him their decision on either hiring or firing him.

"I like how this reception area looks now, Georgio. You have a good eye and good ideas," says John.

"It seems only fair for us to give you a try for a week. Can you type?"

"Yes, sir."

"Now I know what all the hammering was about."

"Well, you told me to tend to the boxes, sir."

"I meant for you to put the books on the shelves that were in the boxes."

"Mario, you didn't tell him that."

"I didn't tell him how to arrange the framed photos and awards either. All these photos are hung at the same height at the top and bottom rows and equally distanced, but I don't recall packing a measuring tape when I packed them, yet they're all in straight rows. How did you accomplish this, Georgio?"

"I used my belt to mark off where the nails should go, sir."

"You did a fine job, Georgio. Get the rest of these boxes unpacked now. You'll be on trial here for a week."

"Welcome to the firm, Georgio. You're our new receptionist."

"Won't I need a typewriter and phone?" "I'll buy you those and a computer, too."

"Thank you, Mr. Fisherkelly. What will my salary be?"

***

Back in Mario's office, John Gilbert slaps him on the back and says, "Good idea you had about buying the computer. I think you now agree with me about this boy?"

"It's only fair to give him a try. He's smart and resourceful, and he can type."

"The coffee he brought to the office this morning was outstanding. He'll soon learn the going price for a receptionist in this building. The figure that he suggested was too low. I think we should increase it before he finds out the going rate. We want to have his trust and friendship. Giving him more money than he asked for should accomplish that. Don't you agree?"

"Yes, we'll give him that, but after his requested salary for the trial week. Then, he'll believe more in his ability to perform here."

"Good point. It may also delay him from asking for a raise in salary before the end of the year."

***

Georgio was pleased to have been given the job, despite that it was on a trial basis. He uses his time riding home on the subway to thank God for leading him to this opportunity in silent prayer.

Chapter 22

Georgio told his mother he believed her coffee was the foot in the door of his job opportunity. Maria blushes and is very pleased to think that in some small way, she'd helped her son to get his job.

***

Things went smoothly at the job and Georgio was accepted as a permanent employee with a raise in his salary. On Sunday afternoon, Georgio thought to call Isabella and thank her for the good advice she'd given him.

Georgio was surprised and concerned after she told him that she'd recognized a new member of the church congregation to be the man who had attacked her.

She'd been careful not to say or do anything to let him know that she recognized him, but now she felt too scared to leave the house. She didn't know what to do about it.

"If I tell my father, I'm sure he would kill him."

"Isabella, you were smart to play it cool. He's a dangerous bad man, but you should go to the police right away and tell them what you just told me."

"You're right. Yes, I must do it. Please, will you come with me when I go?"

"Sure, I'll come over right away. The police will know what to do."

***

Georgio and Isabella were dismayed when the police detective said, "You certainly had a terrible experience, young lady, but when it comes down to it, there was no witness to the crime and it will be your word against his."

***

The following day, Georgio was visibly upset about the lack of a helpful outcome after Isabella had talked to the police, but he went to work anyway and was greeted at the door by Mario.

After one look at Georgio's face, Mario takes him into his office and asks, "Why are you so upset?"

"It shows, huh?"

"All over your face."

Georgio blurts out the whole story to him and sobs that he fears this man will try to kill his friend again.

"That policeman was wrong. There was a witness to what happened."

"What?" exclaimed Georgio.

"Who?" he asks with a puzzled look.

"Isabella's dog was there. He was stabbed too. He knows this man."

"Can a dog testify at a trial?"

"Yes, if it's handled correctly."

"Mr. Fisherkelly, would you help my friend get justice and put this dangerous man in prison?"

"Well, I'd like to help. Let me check my calendar and I'll get back to you later in the day."

***

Georgio immediately calls Isabella to tell her he'd spoken with Mario Fisherkelly. The lawyer that he works for said, "He's pointed out that there was a witness, the dog, and your case should be brought to trial."

John Gilbert overheard Georgio talking to someone when he entered the office on his way to Mario's office to get his morning coffee. On entering, he pours himself a cup, takes a seat, and enquiries, "What's new today?"

"John, Georgio just told me about a horrific attack made on his girlfriend and her dog. She's recovered now. However, yesterday she recognized her assailant, a new member in the church her family attends, but she didn't confront him. Georgio accompanied her to the police station, however, they were told it would only be her word against his word since there was no witness, but her dog was stabbed by the assailant also and therefore a witness. Do you think I should take this case pro bono?"

"Absolutely. Newspaper coverage alone will compensate you for your time and if the dog can point out this man is the assailant in court, that's human-interest stuff. Besides, Georgio's a valuable employee. Now he needs your help. Be a pal to him. You've got everything to gain and nothing to lose."

Mario calls Georgio into his office and tells him to bring in his friend. He is going to take on the case pro bono.

Chapter 23

The day Georgio brought Isabella to his office, Mario was unprepared for his reaction to this beautiful young Italian woman. He tried his best to maintain a professional facade as he listened to her account of what had happened and when she finished, he wanted to beat Otto Hess to a pulp for hurting her.

Mario accepts the case and assures Isabella he will do his best to get her justice.

A few days later, Otto Hess is booked and held for the crime of attempted murder and rape. A switchblade was in his possession when he emptied his pockets, it was sent to the lab for testing.

The telephone on Giorgio's desk was ringing constantly and the schedule of new client appointments on the partners calendar soared.

***

Isabella wanted justice to be done, but she hadn't anticipated the unwanted attention from the press. She phoned Georgio, but he wasn't home. She tearfully confided her complaint to his mom.

Maria listened carefully and was sorry for the girl, so she suggested Isabella might visit a relative until the trial date was set to give her relief from the unwanted attention.

After her suggestion, Isabella asks her mother to call a relative to hide her out for a few days until the trial date.

***

On the witness stand, the defendant, Otto Hess, was asked to state where he'd lived and worked prior to his arrest. After this information was made public in the newspaper, detectives in those areas of the city who had unsolved murder cases where the victim had been raped and her throat slashed took an interest in this case.

They called the precinct to confer with the detective and the prosecuting attorney, Mario Fisherkelly.

Chapter 24

As they'd agreed, each evening when Mario returned to the office, he would tell Georgio what happened in the courtroom. Mario would then tell him how he was going to proceed the following day, thereby giving this future law student an invaluable opportunity to see how this trial lawyer was building his case day by day.

The night before Georgio was to appear in court as a witness, Mario counseled him to be honest and brief when he was called to the stand as a witness.

***

In the courtroom, Georgio was surprised when he was called a "hostile witness" by the defense attorney and told to take the stand.

It was established that Georgio had been at the home of Mr. Wally the night in question. The lawyer questioned Georgio's sexual feelings about Isabella.

Mario objected to this line of questioning and the judge sustained the objection.

However, the defense attorney attempted again to have Georgio admit to strong sexual urges that had gotten beyond his control. Mario jumped to his feet and protested, but Georgio asked the judge if he might answer this question.

"Sir, Isabella is a good friend and I respect her. She's a sweet girl and the daughter of the man I was working for. I would never take advantage of our friendship to attempt to harm her in any way."

From their expressions, it was obvious to Mario that the jury was convinced the boy was telling the truth.

The defense attorney said, "I have no further questions of this witness."

Georgio left the courtroom and headed back to his work at the office. On his way to the train, he was still fuming because of the defense attorney's innuendo that he would violate Isabella.

On board the train, the rocking motion soon calmed him. Georgio understood that the defense attorney was attempting to help his client by throwing suspicion for this crime onto someone else. It was not actually a personal attack on his integrity.

Georgio understood if the lawyer had succeeded in convincing the jury of that possibility then the case against Otto Hess would've been weakened.

***

The following day, photographs of the slashed throat of a few victims were shown. Isabella was asked to show the jury her throat scar, too.

The lab report on the knife Hess carried was submitted which confirmed the victim's blood was there also.

Mario approached the bench to ask that Otto Hess be removed from the court before he called his next witness who was also involved at the crime scene.

The defendant was excused for 10 minutes.

After he was removed, Mario told the jury he was bringing in the only witness to this crime. The door was opened and Isabella's frisky dog was released from his leash.

He ran immediately to his mistress. She pet him and laid at her feet.

Mario walked to the table and dangled the leash. The dog sat up. He then placed the leash on the table and it lay down again. Mario pointed out the dog was calm and aware it was not going to be leashed. He pointed out the dog was calm again to the jury.

Mario signaled to the door to allow a man with a briefcase into the room. The dog lifted its head, but lowered it after the man sat down.

Mario signaled to allow a man playing loud music to enter and sit down. The dog again sat up, but laid down at Isabella's feet.

Mario jiggled the leash and the dog stood up, but Mario put it on the table and the dog lay down. He pointed out to the jury that this dog had been calm about the entry of the two strangers who had come in and sat down.

Mario signaled to allow the defendant to return to the courtroom. He instructed the jury to watch the dog's reaction to the defendant. After that was said, Mario held his breath because he had no idea how this dog was going to react to Hess.

The dog jumped to its feet as Hess came in. The closer he came, the more the dog growled. He didn't bark at him, but instead as Hess came even closer, he whimpered and got under Isabella's chair.

Mario dangled the leash, but the dog wouldn't come out to it. He refused to leave his protection under the chair. It was obvious to everyone that the dog clearly feared Otto.

***

It took the jury 20 minutes to deliberate and come to the verdict of "guilty as charged."

Isabella hugged Mario and thanked him for putting Otto Hess away.

"I now feel safe to walk my dog again."

Sophia insisted Mario come to their house for a victory feast on Saturday night.

***

Mario was taken with Isabella from the moment he saw her. He wanted to protect this innocent girl from any harm from Hess in the future. Mario wanted to come, but he played it cool instead. So, he told her that he had to check his calendar first.

Mario wanted to be certain that there was no romantic involvement with Georgio first for a clear field with Isabella.

She was very different from the kind of wealthy blonde sophisticated women he'd sought as his social equal. However, after two sad experiences with what he'd thought to be "the right woman for him" had failed in his criteria of what he thought he was looking for in a wife, he found Isabella to be a refreshing prospect.

***

During this day, Georgio received many complaints about dirty windows to the attention of Mario Fisherkelly. Georgio was puzzled. He knew Mario was not a window washer.

Later in the afternoon, when Mario returns to the office, he's still elated and quickly shares the events leading up to the testimony of Isabella's dog,

Toby. Georgio is impressed by how cleverly Mario had handled the dog's testimony.

After that, Georgio gave him the dirty window complaints.

Mario sighed, "I've about exhausted the list of specialized tall building window washers."

Georgio suggests, "Why don't you ask Isabella's father to do the job for you? Mr. Wally is a reliable tall building washerman. When I worked for him, he rarely had a complaint."

"Is that so? Georgio, get him on the line for me right now."

He thought, Grandfather will be pleased if I can get someone reliable to handle these complaints quickly.

Georgio knew the number and when Mr. Wally answered, he handed the phone to Mario.

"This is Mario Fisherkelly, Mr. Wally."

"Yes, what can I do for you?"

"I'm your daughter's lawyer."

"Oh! Thank you for defending my daughter, I'll pay you whatever you ask…"

"I'm not calling to tell you what you owe me, sir."

"Hmmn!"

"I understand that you specialize in cleaning the windows of tall buildings and would like to contract you to clean the Fisher building right away. How soon can you start?"

"I'll need to check my calendar."

"Meantime sir, may I speak to your wife?"

"I happen to be home, give me a minute and I'll get her."

Mario turns and says, "Georgio, I was invited to have dinner with them Saturday night."

"Sophia is a great cook, you'll enjoy it."

"Hello Sophia, I find that I'm free this Saturday and I'm happy to accept your invitation."

Georgio closes the door as he leaves Mario's office and returns to his desk. He's pleased with the outcome of Isabella's case and hopes that one day he will become as good a lawyer as his employer.

Chapter 25

Mario Fisherkelly is speaking on the phone in his office to his grandfather, "With all the publicity and success from the case I just won, the phone has been ringing off the hook."

"I saw how you handled yourself in court, Mario. I slipped in and out of the court unnoticed many times. Now that you've proved yourself as a good lawyer, you're going to be very busy."

"That's what I wanted to talk to you about, Grandfather."

"What do you have in mind?"

"There's a receptionist kid that I've hired who is as sharp as a tack. I feel he would be perfect for managing the building. He has proved himself to be able to take initiative, and his problem-solving skills are extraordinary. He was the one who recommended Mr. Wally to me to clean the building's windows."

"Sounds like a possible fit, Mario. What is this young lad's name?"

"Georgio."

"Oh, that young man from the trial. I'll set him up for an interview with me. I'll meet him casually to feel him out, before I advertise to fill your old position. Just in case, I feel he might be too young or inexperienced, after all, not being my grandson who needs to have a job, I won't have time to show him the ropes. Being the chief superintendent of a building is a very demanding job as you've learned over the years with my guidance."

"I know the lessons I've learned from you in solving problems over the years have helped me work my way through law school."

"Yes! We've had some good times together. Your parent's laid the foundation for you to remain teachable before they died. I know they would be just as proud of you as I am."

"Thanks Grandfather, it's at times like this that I truly miss them. I wish I could celebrate my success with them."

"Their murder still haunts me. I'm glad you nailed that bastard, Hess, who harmed that pretty girl."

"After mom and dad's murder and the injustice that followed, it made it easy for me to find my calling as a lawyer."

"I'm glad that God has blessed me with good health and a position where I could help you. It's been great working with you, Mario."

"Hey, remember the earthquake that had us believing that the boiler had exploded?"

"Boy, that had us going. I'll tell you what, I'll stop by while he's working and see how Georgio treats me informally. Then, if I like him, I'll set up an interview for the following week."

"Sounds good, but that young man can be pretty resourceful. He's liable to come up with something else that could surprise us both."

"I am intrigued now. I'll see you soon, bye now."

"Bye."

Mario hangs up the phone and calls Georgio on the office intercom.

"I want to tell you that we like you but, I must point out to you that a receptionist salary is not enough to put you through your law studies. I want to make you aware of this so that you can consider making arrangements before college starts. I was once in your position. However, I was lucky enough to have a wealthy grandfather," but he insisted that I go to school at night and work for him during the day as the building manager's assistant until I could do it solo.

Georgio, I want you to know that we're interested in your welfare and I'm trying to work out a possible solution to your problem. I don't want you to feel like you're standing alone."

"Mr. Fisherkelly, I'm appreciative of what you're trying to do for me, but I have a scholarship. I'm also considering taking out a student loan."

"Well, if what I'm working on comes through, you may not have to worry about a student loan to have to contend with after you graduate. So, promise me that you'll keep an open mind to what I'm working on."

"I'm open to all future possibilities. Thank you, Mr. Fisherkelly."

***

A few days later, Edward Fishkelly enters the office to take his grandson for lunch. He sees Georgio eating his lunch while he's manning the phones at the reception desk.

Georgio recognizes the grandfather of his boss and wipes his mouth with a napkin and says, "Good morning, Mr. Fisherkelley. How can I help you?"

The surprised man asks, "How do you know who I am?"

"I recognized you from the photographs of you hugging your grandson at his graduation from college and law school."

"Mario told me that you were a smart boy, but now I see for myself that you're a truly bright young man."

"What can I do for you, sir."

Georgio wipes his hand and accepts Mr. Fisherkelley's hand to shake. Edward thinks to himself, I would like to meet this young man's father. I'll bet he's brilliant to have a son like this young man.

"I'm impressed that you were able to recognize me, so I'll come to the point. My grandson suggested that you replace his position with me. He's the superintendent of this building. Mario worked by day while attending night school to get his degree. If you're interested, then you could do the same. I want to have an in-depth conversation with you and your parents. Are you interested?"

"I can see this is a wonderful opportunity, sir. However, I'll have to pray on it to see if it's right for me. I hope to have my answer when we meet again."

"Write down your address and I'll have my driver pick you and your parents up at 11:30 this Sunday."

Georgio quickly writes down his address and hands it to him.

"Here you are, sir."

"You can tell my grandson that I'm here."

"Yes, sir."

Georgio announces on the intercom that his grandfather is here while Edward puts Georgio's address in his jacket pocket.

"I'll be right there," is heard on the intercom.

***

A smiling Georgio walks into the kitchen where his parents are seated at the table.

"You look like you have some good news to share. What's up?"

"Papa, you've always said that God works in mysterious ways. I believe what's happening right now is one of them."

"What do you mean, Georgio?"

"Yes, what is it?" asks Mama.

"My boss suggested to his grandfather that he interview me to replace him as superintendent of the Fisher building."

"That big building downtown?" asks Carlos.

"Yes, and he's sending a driver to pick us up to have lunch with him this Sunday at 11:30 with your permission, Papa."

"Okay, we can go to early mass and be ready for his car by 11:30, Georgio."

"Papa, that's not all I'm thinking about. The job I'm interviewing for is to be the superintendent of the Fisher building."

Maria gasps and says, "But what about you being a lawyer?"

"My boss told me that he went to school at night and worked during the day. He wants me to have the same opportunity that he did."

Carlos asks, "That sounds very nice, so what's wrong?"

"Papa, it would mean living at the Fisher building like him. If I'm working by day and going to school at night, I'll have no time to come and see you and Mama. It would break up our family life."

Mama gets teary eyed, "My baby boy's growing up."

"What do you hope to see in this meeting, Georgio?" asks his father.

"Our family should stick together and not drift apart. You are far more qualified for this job of superintendent than I am."

"He has a point," says Maria.

"What are you trying to say, Georgio?"

"Papa, this is an important job. If I'm not able to do it, it may be that God wants you to have this job, then we can all stay together."

"Ah, I see what you're saying. I have the experience this job requires."

"Papa, Mr. Fisherkelly is big on a family working together. Once he finds out what you do for a living, I'm sure that he'll want you for this job, then I'll be able to remain at the law office part time. I've learned a lot about the practice of law from Mario already."

"Well, I guess we'll have to wait for Sunday to see what the Lord will unfold."

Papa joins hands with Georgio and Mama and says, "Let us give our thanks to the Lord for this opportunity."

***

Seated in Central Park at "Tavern on the Green," Edward Fisherkelly sits relaxed on the patio at his favorite restaurant. He reads his Sunday newspaper while under a shady tree at a table.

Turning a page, he glances up at the road and sees his limousine turn the curve that leads to the front of the restaurant.

He's aware that the doorman will welcome them and the maitre d' will escort Georgio and his parents to his table.

As the limo pulls up to the curb, Maria is surprised and says, "This is a big house in the park."

"No, Maria. See that sign? This is a restaurant."

The doorman recognizes Mr. Fisherkelly's driver and opens their door. He then directs the guests of Mr. Fisherkelly to the maitre d' who then shows them to the table of Mr. Fisherkelly who is seated, awaiting his guests.

***

Ed Fisherkelly folds his newspaper on seeing Georgio coming toward the table with his parents. He rises and extends his hand to Georgio and his parents.

"I'm Carlos Lopez, this is my wife, Maria."

"Very nice to meet you both. Please be seated."

The waiter gives each of them a menu.

"The fish here is top notch," says their host. "I recommend the red snapper, but you're welcome to choose whatever you like from the menu."

***

Fruit cups are brought to the table for each of them. Carlos is quick to bow his head and fold his hands in prayer, "Thank you, Lord, for this good food. Amen."

Everyone else responds with "Amen."

"I see you're a man of faith, Mr. Lopez. I'm curious, what livelihood did you choose?"

"I worked as the general manager of a small department store for 18 years. However, when the owner's son was old enough to join the family business, he fired me. I was upset and didn't know what direction to take.

Fortunately, my clever Maria had anticipated this catastrophe was going to happen, so she wrote to her brother about us coming to the States. He agreed to assist us.

When we got here, he helped me to examine my job skills for employment here. Well…I had to fix everything in our rented house in Puerto Rico, the plumbing, electricity, and carpentry because the owner wouldn't do it for us.

"Sounds like you've had a rough adventure, Carlos. What happened next?"

"I would say that God took over after that. One day, I was searching through the newspaper for a job. Later on, I happened to walk by a building that looked like it badly needed repairs. I was going in there to inquire about it just as the landlord was having his drunken superintendent removed from the building by the police. Well, I offered my services to him and he gave me the job. I've been there now for two years."

"How many apartments are in that building?"

"50."

The spoon slips from Edward's hand and hits the plate. His eyes open wide and he says, "Mr. Lopez, I need a superintendent badly. Would you consider working for me?"

"What do you mean?"

"I got so caught up in your story that I felt like I had become a part of it."

Georgio suggests, "Mr. Fisherkelly, sir, you need to hire my father as the new superintendent of your building, he's the best man for this job. Then I'll be able to stay on with your grandson and hope to prove myself an asset to you all."

"You make a good case, Georgio, but we haven't heard from your father on this matter."

"Sir, I've heard from my son that family means a lot to you, too. I want to continue to preserve the integrity of my family. If the position you offer has an apartment included for us, then my answer is yes."

"How long did you say you've been working for your current employer, Mr. Lopez?"

"The place was a mess when I started there, a little over two years ago, but now everything's running tiptop."

"Have you done any boiler repair?"

"I've been doing some maintenance as a preventive measure and it's fine?"

"How did you learn to work with a boiler?"

"I got my coaching from the parish priest after I asked him if he knew anything about it from maintaining his Church. He told me to call the Stirling Boiler Company, so I purchased their manual and read through it a few times. After that, I called the company for confirmation to check out if I was doing it right."

"I like a man who shows initiative and knows how to handle himself."

I learned from my first employer, "We can do all things through Christ who strengthens us."

"Amen to that."

Carlos smiles when Edward extends his hand to him and says, "Welcome aboard."

Carlos replies, "I'll give my employer notice right away, but I won't leave him until he has made other arrangements for someone to help him."

"Fair enough." They shake hands.

***

Corto sees Georgio helping his dad load a moving truck in front of their building. He recognizes that the furniture is from the Lopez apartment. He rushes to tell Josh. He becomes enraged and lashes out at Edwardo seated next to him and pushes him off the park wall they are sitting on.

"Did you get me the stuff, man?"

Corto replies, "Yeah, I got it right here!"

"Don't take it out, man. You'll get us busted! Don't you know there's a detective in the park?"

Corto asks, "Should we go to the cave?"

"Come on, bright boy."

Edwardo, realizing now he's lying in the bushes, shouts, "What did ya do that for?"

Josh pulls out his switchblade and brandishes it, "You don't like something."

Corto intervenes, "Put it away, man, before somebody sees. Come on, let's go to the cave. Remember, I got the stash, man."

***

Georgio appears just before they leave the park while Josh mouths off to him, "Just because you're moving doesn't mean you're out of the gang. Beat it now! I'll deal with you later."

While they're walking away, Josh continues mouthing off, "He's just lucky he showed up."

***

Later on, Josh, Edwardo and Corto show up at the moving truck just as the door rolls down and is locked shut by Mr. Lopez. He sees them and calls to his son,

"Georgio, I see your friends have come to say goodbye."

"I'll be over in a minute, Papa" He climbs down out of the cab from the passenger side of the truck.

His father climbs into the cab and closes the driver's door.

Josh asks, "So, where ya moving to, Georgio?" "Downtown."

"Don't get smart with me!"

"Hey, why are you saying that, Josh? You cut me off in the middle of my sentence."

"Just remember who was there for ya when you needed help."

"Josh, you're speaking gibberish. You really don't look so good either. What's going on with you?"

"You think you're better than us because you're moving?"

"Hey, I'm still part of the gang. You treated me right, so I'll do the same for you. I'll call you as soon as I get our new phone number."

"Yeah, sure. Now get outta here. Don't keep your old man waiting."

Georgio starts walking towards the front of the truck and Josh calls out, "Hey, what's your new address?"

He shouts back the address and gets into the truck which slowly pulls away.

Edwardo speaks up, "Doesn't he still have to come to meetings?"

"We'll pay him a visit and collect the dues if he don't show up next week."

Corto agrees with Josh, "Hey, that's a great idea. Anyone who doesn't show up for meetings should pay a fine instead of getting a beating from us from now on."

Josh gives him a long look, "I like that. Perhaps, you've become the brains around here now."

Edwardo asks Josh, "Speaking of money, how much bank do we have? I'm starving."

Josh replies, "We have enough. Come on, let's get some lunch."

***

Josh is lying in bed when he hears the phone. "Hello?"

"Hi, Josh. It's me, Georgio. If you have a pen handy, I'll give you my home phone number. Most likely you'll have to leave a message on the answering machine and I'll call you back."

"Georgio, my message to you is, if you don't want to show up for meetings each week, you can mail me $20 instead to avoid any beatings."

"What I'm going to be offering you in legal advice is far more valuable than any dues money. You're trying to get money from me for your drugs. I recall how strung out you were the last time I saw you, Josh. Get to a rehab and call me. I'll pay for you to get off that stuff. If you don't, there's one of three places you're gonna end up if you don't kick your drug habit."

"And where would that be?"

"Take my phone number and address first because you're not thinking clearly and you're likely to hang up on me when I tell you."

"Alright, I got a pen and paper."

"My phone number is 718-784-2433. I'm in the superintendent's apartment, Fisher Building 229 Broadway."

"Got it. Now what?"

"You're going to end up dead, in jail, or in a psych ward."

"I'm taking that as you're gonna renege on paying up your dues…"

"I didn't say that."

"Some things not said speak louder without saying them! I'll be in touch." He hangs up the phone on him.

***

The doorbell rings at Josh's apartment and he gets up. Zig-zagging his way to the door, he opens it after asking, "Who's there?"

"It's Corto. I'm here with the new shipment."

Removing the chain from the door after two failed attempts, he lets Shorty into his room. Corto looks at the chaos in the apartment and says, "Man, you gotta stop using! Those free samples have you and your place all messed up!"

"Shut up! I don't need to hear that from you, too. That no good Georgio is trying to cross us by saying that stuff to me."

"Cross us? What do you mean?"

"He doesn't want to pay up!"

"Hey, wait a minute, Josh. It's Friday, right?"

"Yeah! That's right, what of it?"

"It's the night his old man always collects his pay envelope from the landlord. He always gets paid in cash."

"Is that so?!"

"I say we jump the old man and get his money and call it even. That'll hurt Georgio worse 'cause he'll know he's the one who caused his Papa to get hurt."

"Great idea, brains!"

"Come on, let's go get Edwardo."

"What do we need him for? There'll be more money for us without him."

"It's gonna take the three of us. I heard his old man was once a fighter."

"All right. We'll get Edwardo, but then what?"

"We can lay low by the entrance to the subway station. He's got to come by that way. You watch the subway station and see when he comes while I go get Edwardo."

***

Josh and Edwardo meet up with Corto at the subway entrance and ask, "Has he passed by yet?"

"Yeah. It's almost 5 o'clock. He came by about 10 minutes ago. I heard the sound of his keys jingling as he passed by me. I thought you guys would never show up."

Josh says, "Corto, you get down the stairs and when he passes by, hit him with this," he hands him a black jack.

"I'll be right behind you. If he turns to see who hit him, I'll deck him with my brass knuckles. He'll go down for sure after that."

"Won't he recognize us?" asks Edwardo.

"Not to worry, he'll be blinded momentarily as he's coming down the stairs out of the bright sunlight when he enters the tunnel."

"You get the money while he's down, Edwardo."

"Then what?"

"We'll go pay Georgio a little visit by train."

Corto reminds Josh, "Hey, we agreed after we robbed his dad that we'd let him go from the gang."

"I changed my mind."

***

"Wow! Look at all those keys," says Edwardo as Carlos Lopez comes into sight.

"Get those keys, too, while he's down. He must already be the superintendent of the Fisher building."

"How do you know that?" asks Edwardo.

"Because that's where Georgio said he's at," replies Josh.

"Now, let's go down some stairs to make it look like we just came out of the train station. After he passes us, we'll turn and follow him."

***

Later on, they leave the subway at 229 Broadway. Josh realizes while talking to the gang, "With the keys, we can score big here. It's getting dark, take these dimes, Edwardo, and call everyone in the gang to meet here." He runs to the pay phone.

"I don't understand this," says Corto.

"We're gonna frame Georgio."

"How?"

"He's the only one who can borrow his father's keys. After we help ourselves, he'll get the blame. At least until his dad gets out of the hospital."

"Did you have to hit him so hard with those brass knuckles of yours?"

"That's only because you didn't hit him hard enough with the black jack."

"I don't feel right about this. I like Mr. Lopez."

"Are you going soft on me when we've got the keys to the kingdom of riches?" He holds the keys up and dangles them before him.

Edwardo comes running. After catching up, he speaks while catching his breath, "I called the rest of the gang and told them to meet us in the lobby right away."

"Let's go borrow a moving van from my uncle. He parks them near here. After the gang gets here, we'll ransack the offices till we fill the truck for tonight's job."

***

Just before 9:00 pm, Edwardo shows up with the van and the other gang members. They stop in front of the building, "Give me those keys," says Josh.

"It's party time."

***

Carlos Lopez is lying quietly in a hospital bed when his wife and son come in to see him. Maria becomes choked up with emotion when she sees her husband in the bed and sobs aloud. Carlos hears her and slowly opens his eyes.

"Carlos, I'm so worried about you." She goes over and takes his hand.

Georgio brings over a chair for his mother to sit on and says, "We prayed for you, Papa."

"They caught me by surprise, Georgio."

Maria says, "It's over now and you're still with us, thank God. That's what counts."

"They caught them, Papa. They saw them in the act of robbing the offices on the security cameras, and called the police. The police were able to capture all of them. The entire crime was recorded on tape."

***

A detective is going over the Pinkerton reel which reveals the gang going on a rampage through the offices of the Fisher building and are caught taking the petty cash from one of the offices as the police enter the scene. Afterward, he goes to the police chief to give his report.

"We have enough evidence on tape to put those hoodlums away for a long time."

"I'll call the DA's office right away, this should be an open and shut case."

"Chief, there's one other thing."

"What?"

"They had the keys to the building with them. This may have been an inside job."

"Get on it."

"Yes, sir."

***

Two detectives are questioning Georgio. The first officer is straightforward, "How did the gang get the keys to get into the Fisher building, Georgio? Rumor has it that you know the boys who broke into the building. Do you know how they got the keys? Fess up and it will go easy on you."

I just came from visiting my father in the hospital who was beaten and robbed. I'm very upset. My dad carried his keys with pride. Papa is proud to be the new superintendent of the Fisher building. Perhaps they got them from him when he was robbed.

"You set up your father. How else could the gang have known where he'd be?"

"I love my Papa, I would never set him up to get hurt."

"So, you admit that you'd set him up if he didn't get hurt. It's known that you're with them, we have witnesses."

Georgio's tears run down his cheeks.

"I'm sick over this, leave me alone."

The other detective offers him water, "Here, drink some water, you'll feel better. We're only trying to help your father by solving this case, Georgio. If you cooperate with us, we can get to the bottom of this sooner than later."

"I told you, I don't know anything, but I do know that I am here without parental consent. I know my rights, you cannot hold me."

"Now, how would you know that unless you've been picked up before?" asks the first detective.

"I work in a law office and you need to let me go."

The two detectives talk quietly together in a corner of the room and return.

The nice detective says, "You're free to go. Thanks for coming in, we'll be in touch."

"Don't leave town." says the other detective in a gruff voice.

Georgio says, "Why would I leave when I live with my parents?"

The nice detective opens the door before Georgio leaves.

***

In the jail holding tank, Josh is starting to feel the effects of withdrawal. Now "dope sick," he breaks out in a sweat and hugs himself trying to keep warm. Another prisoner comments on his condition, "Hah! Look at the freak," he says to the detainee sitting next to him.

Edwardo goes to Josh and stands directly in front of him, "Can't you see he's sick, man?"

"You want some trouble?"

Corto gets up from sitting on the ground in the pen and stands to tower over to them and says, "Seeing that we're all in here for circumstances beyond our control, I think we should try to get along."

The brazen detainee looks up to Corto and takes his suggestion, "I like your idea," he says in a squeaky voice.

"Really, I do."

Josh starts to dry heave and throws up on the floor.

***

The chief of police calls the two detectives taking care of the Lopez case into his office and says, "I have something here that I want you two to see."

They sit down in the room and look at the tape on a television monitor of three boys at the subway station. Corto, Josh, and Edward were caught in action as they beat and robbed Carlos Lopez.

The camera at the train station not only caught this, but the removal of the man's keys from his belt as well.

The two detectives look at each other at the same time and say, "That boy was telling us the truth."

The nice detective says while looking at his partner, "I'll get Mr. Lopez's statement at the hospital."

"I'll speak with Georgio's mother to see if his alibi checks out," says the other detective.

Chapter 26

At the hospital, Georgio is having a long overdue conversation with his father, "Papa, I knew that you and mama had to work, so I didn't tell you that I got beat up a lot at school. I didn't want you to worry about me. Then, I joined a gang for my protection and everyone stopped bothering me."

"Georgio, I don't want you to blame yourself for what happened to me. You've always chosen to do the right thing. I taught you as a child and you know how to listen to reason. The gang must have noticed this when you stopped smoking marijuana, that's what really matters. You know when you do the right thing, good things will happen, wait and see."

"You're right, Papa. God has shown me favor because of it."

"I know that you're angry with the boys in your gang right now for what they did to me, but pray to God and you'll find that place in your heart where you can forgive them. I know that you want revenge right now, but remember that "vengeance is mine," says the Lord."

Georgio hears a fire truck pass by and gets distracted before turning back to continue to listen to his father.

"I know that this burden lays heavily upon you, but don't take action against them to avenge me. I'm sure it will only lead to trouble in your future. Do the right thing by God, my son, or you'll end up hardening your heart and breaking mine."

Georgio takes his father's hand and says, "Papa, I'll go to Church as soon as I leave you." He continues to sit by his father's side.

"Drugs have a way of taking over a person to where they're not themselves anymore, Georgio. I'm sure that you must have seen the changes in your friends since you stopped smoking."

"Yes, Papa. I've seen a big difference."

"There is good in everyone, my son, it just needs to be brought out. Now please, I want you to guard your heart and pray for those boys who attacked me until you can forgive them, the same way God has forgiven you."

"But shouldn't there be consequences for their actions?"

"That's for the law to decide. I want you to continue to do the right thing and all will go well for you."

"I will pray about it, Papa."

"Good. Please go tell Mama I want to see her now."

***

After Georgio tells his mother his dad wants to see her, he walks down the hall to the chapel in the hospital and walks in. He kneels down on his knees before the tabernacle and seeks guidance, quieting himself before the Lord.

He says, "God, after all that has happened, you have my full attention. What do you want of me?"

At first, all he can hear is the large grandfather clock ticking in the quiet room. He then remembers what the priest had told him, "God has three answers when praying: wait, yes or no."

"Calm now", Georgio is able to quiet himself by waiting on the still presence of God.

He now discovers that his love is deeper than before. Georgio's focus is guided to ponder through his thoughts about this situation till feeling embraced from within.

Searching his path, he discovers the truth of his situation by connecting to God's vine of love in the Tree of Life.

Drawing from this understanding of life, he's taken on a journey, enabling him to search his mind selflessly.

"Lord, I feel crossed by my gang. Why should I try to help them?"

What's that? How is it that when I was without understanding, you could still love me until I found your spiritual brilliance.

"I had no one to help me while I was getting beat up in school"

Was that part of your plan for me? You wanted me to join this gang, then arranged it for me to work for a law firm so I could help the gang get out of trouble later on? I think I understand now. They've had no one to direct them all their lives while I've been blessed with my good family.

If I don't help them now, they'll have no one to guide them to turn themselves around...

"So, now I understand. You want me to be used as a guide for them to try a different way to live their lives without the gang."

"What would You have me do?

Chapter 27

Georgio is manning the phones in the office at lunchtime. His father stops in to see him carrying a brown paper bag which he gives to him and says, "Mama made something special for lunch, so I figured that I'd share some of it with you."

"Thanks, Papa."

He opens the bag and takes out two medium sized teflon bowls and removes their lids to see what's for lunch. The first bowl has a nice salad with ginger dressing. He discovers chicken and olive rice with spices in the second bowl. He gives thanks to the Lord, finds a fork, and begins to eat.

His dad says, "Georgio, I was praying this morning and a question came to my mind: have you visited your old gang members in jail?"

"Papa, I've been so busy here, I just didn't have any spare time to go."

Carlos Lopez gives his son a look that says, "It's time."

"Okay, Papa. You're right, I will go and see them this Saturday."

***

At the county jail, Georgio walks along the circular path with lots of windows in a large room until he finds the correct number. He sits down in a visiting cubicle and waits. On the other side of the glass window is a small speaker to talk through in the center and an empty chair

A short time later, he observes inmates starting to fill the windows until Corto finally arrives and sits down.

Georgio says, "How are things going?"

"What are you doing here?"

"Trying to help."

"Why'd you leave us in here to rot?"

"Why did you jump my Papa?"

"Josh said you crossed us and that the best way to get back at you was to hurt your papa."

"Corto, when are you going to learn to hear your own voice? You put yourself in here because you listened to Josh who would easily turn on his own mother."

"Then what took you so long to come and see me?"

"I had to pray hard on whether or not to see any of you again. After that, I had to wait for you guys to sober up and let you get your mind drug-free."

"You gonna help me now?"

"First, you and the others have to help yourselves."

"What do you mean?"

"I've learned that if you want a reduced sentence and time off for good behavior, you should take advantage of getting your GED. I also understand they have a work program to learn a trade while you're in prison. Do it."

"I will."

"When you're up for parole, I'll try my best to help you all to get jobs."

"What kind of job should I learn?"

"Corto, you're too tall to be a plumber, so try to learn about electrical repair... if you can."

"I'll look into it."

"How are the others?

Turning his head, Corto sucks in his gut before looking back.

He shares the news, "Josh is dead!"

"Dead! What happened to him?"

"He got some bad stuff in here and overdosed."

"It's hard to believe that Josh is dead."

"Believe it."

A loud buzzer sounds and Corto announces, "I gotta go."

"Hey, tell Edwardo to take up plumbing."

"Will do."

He starts getting up to walk back to his cell.

Seven years later...

Chapter 28

Georgio is now a lawyer sitting at his desk at the new law offices of Mario Fisherkelly.

A few moments later, Georgio hears his intercom, "Georgio, can you come into my office please."

"I'm on my way."

Rising from his desk, he hurries to Mario's office. Upon entering, he sees a pale Mario and Edward Fisherkelley. They look as if they've just seen a ghost. He closes the door behind him.

Edward lets his mind be known, "I'll get right to the point. Georgio, what were you thinking when you suggested to the parole board that the men who ransacked my building would be hired here?"

"Sir, the fact they got time off for good behavior proves they've learned to honor set rules.

They were misguided and confused youngsters when they were arrested following the orders of their gang leader.

These young men need jobs now. They've completed their GEDs and have taken classes to learn to perform jobs that will be useful here for low pay.

Let's give them a break. If given jobs here, they can prove to us and themselves that they're just as valuable now as anyone else. A chance to make amends and earn an honest livelihood will meet a need for everyone. Otherwise, they may lose interest in honest work at real jobs and revert to their old ways of easy living.

Edward further questions, "But why my building and not somewhere else?"

Mario speaks in a reprimanding way, "Why did your father hire them to work here of all places?"

Georgio replies, "If not us then who is going to get them out of their former lifestyle of crime? I know these men want a chance to prove themselves. If my father can forgive them for beating and robbing him, then why can't they be forgiven for trying to steal here?"

The grandfather and Mario stare at one another and then to Georgio who has spoken so altruistically. They are unable to refute him on any level.

Georgio continues, "Look, at first I wanted revenge on the gang, but my dad encouraged me to forgive them by pointing out that they had been misguided by bad leadership.

They lacked faith in God and the golden rule. The so-called good things in life was all that they wanted, but were unwilling to learn jobs to get them.

No one else has cared about them up till now. A lack of knowing that God blesses us for doing the right thing is what steered them in the wrong direction in the first place.

We know that very few people will give them a chance to prove themselves, that's what moved me to help them. They've paid their debt to society and have rehabilitated themselves.

You'll inspire other companies to give such men a second chance. Give them this opportunity to prove themselves.

Be advised, reporting to their parole officer on a regular basis is a part of the plan. If there's any infraction, they will return to prison."

Edward nods his head and says, "I see what you're saying as I've heard it said, "No good deed goes unpunished."

Georgio says, "God moves in mysterious ways. I'll use myself as an example to you."

Edward responds, "What you've said so far resonates with me. Go ahead."

"I became a member of the gang because I sought their protection when my family came to the States. I could have ended up just like them if it had not been for my father's intervention.

I joined the gang because I was beaten, abused, and bullied at school and on the street. When I joined them, I gave them my word as a member that I would always help them. My integrity of being a worker for you is just as important to me as the pledge that I gave to my gang.

It's like you, sir, assuming the role of father to your grandson when his parents were murdered."

Edward protests, "That was different."

"Is it? Our Father in heaven loves all his children. Don't we all want to be treated the same way? We love and serve Him the way He would like for us to love all our brothers and sisters.

My gang members have repented while in prison by learning how to do helpful jobs which shows they've mended their ways. They've cleaned up the windows of their minds and attitudes through the work of God. Completing their GEDs and learning to do a variety of useful skills, they've made themselves become employable.

If we don't give them a chance to use their new work ethics now and be able to change for better tomorrows, then we damn them to the bitter dregs of a poor future for all."

Both men were stunned after listening to his plea. Mario says, "Georgio, you're a fine lawyer and you've stated your case with good motivation. I can't refute your logic, but I still feel uneasy about it."

"In this life, sir, there is always uncertainty. When we deal with people, thinking they're good and when it turns out that they're not, we learn patience because we suffer the fact they're not trustworthy with each disappointment.

On the other hand, we rejoice when those who were thought of as unworthy do well because we gave them the opportunity to prove themselves and here, all become rewarded by the fact that they can."

"I understand. You're saying that 'God works all things for good for those who love Him.'"

"Yes, it requires being a friend to make a friend. This is what pleases God and uplifts everyone to feel good in the end."

Edward looks relieved and says, "I better understand now why you are pleading for these men. In the past, I've noticed you have always done your best. You're a friend and wouldn't advise me to do anything that wasn't in my best interest."

"Sir, thank you for your confidence in me, I now feel that justice will be served for all."

Milton Keynes UK
Ingram Content Group UK Ltd.
UKHW021901131024
449515UK00003B/9